Praise for *The Chaos*

"Gordon White writes fabulously well in a very engagingly opinionated way. He has brought Chaos magic out of the retro chic niche that was slightly endangering it and has made it thoroughly modern, immediately usable, and dynamic again. He slays economic theory as taught and accepted, and the section doing that prepares the reader for a re-think of how and why they want to do magic. Any book that gives achievable, repeatable methods is useful; one where you know why is even more so."

—Geraldine Beskin, proprietor of the Atlantis Bookshop

"Gordon's writing never fails to impress, but to see his talents applied to a topic as imperative as navigating these troubled times with a full wizardly toolbox? Well, that's a beautiful thing."

—Greg Carlwood, host of *The Higherside Chats*

THE
CHAOS
PROTOCOLS

About the Author

Gordon White (London) runs one of the leading chaos magic blogs, *Rune Soup*. He has worked nationally and internationally for some of the world's largest digital and social media companies, including BBC Worldwide, Discovery Channel, and Yelp. Gordon has presented at media events across Europe on social strategy and the changing behaviors and priorities of Generation Y. During this time, he has partied with princes, dined in castles, been mentored by a former director of a private spy agency, and even had a billionaire knight buy him bottles of champagne.

To Write the Author

If you wish to contact the author or would like more information about this book, please write to the author in care of Llewellyn Worldwide, and we will forward your request. Both the author and the publisher appreciate hearing from you and learning of your enjoyment of this book and how it has helped you. Llewellyn Worldwide cannot guarantee that every letter written to the author can be answered, but all will be forwarded. Please write to:

Gordon White
℅ Llewellyn Worldwide
2143 Wooddale Drive
Woodbury, MN 55125-2989

Please enclose a self-addressed stamped envelope for reply,
or $1.00 to cover costs. If outside the USA, enclose
an international postal reply coupon.

Many of Llewellyn's authors have websites with additional information and resources. For more information, please visit www.llewellyn.com.

THE
CHAOS
PROTOCOLS

MAGICAL TECHNIQUES FOR NAVIGATING
THE NEW ECONOMIC REALITY

GORDON WHITE

Llewellyn Publications
Woodbury, Minnesota

First Edition
Fourth Printing, 2018

Book design by Bob Gaul
Chapter opener art by Llewellyn Art Department
Cover art by iStockphoto.com/9370966/©wepix
          iStockphoto.com/10549465/©cajoer
          iStockphoto.com/13898478/©quantum_orange
          iStockphoto.com/14893197/©ziggymaj
Cover design by Kevin R. Brown
Editing by Laura Graves

Llewellyn Publications is a registered trademark of Llewellyn Worldwide Ltd.

Library of Congress Cataloging-in-Publication Data
Names: White, Gordon, 1981– author.
Title: The chaos protocols : magical techniques for navigating the new
   economic reality / Gordon White.
Description: First Edition. | Woodbury : Llewellyn Worldwide, Ltd, 2016. |
   Includes bibliographical references and index.
Identifiers: LCCN 2015044365 (print) | LCCN 2016002237 (ebook) | ISBN
   9780738744711 | ISBN 9780738747477 ()
Subjects: LCSH: Magic. | Civilization—21st century—Miscellanea.
Classification: LCC BF1621 .W45 2016 (print) | LCC BF1621 (ebook) | DDC
   133.4/3—dc23
LC record available at http://lccn.loc.gov/2015044365

Llewellyn Publications
A Division of Llewellyn Worldwide Ltd.
2143 Wooddale Drive
Woodbury, MN 55125-2989
www.llewellyn.com

Printed in the United States of America

CONTENTS

INTRODUCTION

The problem is not to find the answer, it's to face the answer.

TERENCE MCKENNA

Sometimes I go to the Hall of Asian Antiquities in the British Museum, sit on a bench, and think about the Kali Yuga. According to the Mahabharata, the great Hindu epic, this is the age in which we currently live. As a two-thousand-year-old description of the modern world, it is unsurpassed in its dismal accuracy. Spiritual teachers are mocked, rulers no longer see it as their duty to protect their citizens and become a danger to the whole world, dramatic climate shocks kill us by the thousands, millions die hungry. There are even descriptions of great metal birds bringing death that we assumed were airplanes but are probably, with the benefit of unenviable hindsight, military drones. According to the yuga system, to be born during the Kali Yuga is to have the most challenging incarnation possible. Yet here we are! Congratulations on your amazing timing.

The Asian Antiquities Hall is a particularly unloved corner of the British Museum and it shows. Its treasures are almost sheepishly displayed,

1

under glass and with quiet little cards next to them, as if the last hundred years of cultural studies never happened. The hall has none of the inspiring confidence or wonderful bombast you see in the museum's other wings. There are no touch screens or holographic projections here. These are relics not only from a culture that thought it would last forever and is now vanished but are also *displayed* by a culture that thought it had worked out how to avoid vanishing and is also now largely obliterated. Sitting on the first floor at the back of the museum where comparatively few people venture, there is something awkwardly hand-wringing about the collection. It reminds me of those alarmingly racist relics from a different era, like the inherited *objet* your family hides away in your grandmother's attic—too controversial to put in the sitting room, too valuable to put on eBay.

To me, this says everything about the modern era. The British Museum is, without question, my favourite place on earth. It is free to enter. Millions pass through its doors each year. Past its three gift shops, two restaurants and up the back stairs are some profound objects hiding in plain view. No great quests into the Himalayas are required. These artefacts could not be more readily accessible to anyone who is interested. If you but take the time to just *look* and *think* then your life might just change forever. Few take that time.

You may be aware that the term *samsāra* refers to the continuous circle of incarnations through the various worlds for those that have not yet reached enlightenment. Its original etymology means "perpetual wandering." Like visitors through a museum, we wander from gallery to gallery. I'll be happy when I get that promotion. I'll devote time to my spirituality when I have paid off my credit card. The Buddha's solution is for us to give up attachment, to give up striving. This is sound advice in a world where you would stay a peasant if you were born a peasant. No amount of desire could turn you into a prince. But we live in a world where, at least in theory, one can accomplish great things regardless of their birth status. A new method of dealing with perpetual wandering is required in a world where there still may be even the slightest hope that you can accomplish great things with your incarnation.

Magic is always the tactic of last resort for those who refuse to give up hope. You do not summon Cthulhu to help you find the TV remote. You only visit the witch at the edge of the village when all other options have been explored, for she is the loan shark of the gods. It is only a certain kind of person who is willing to take the road we are about to walk. This book is written for that person. For the person who, when life gives them lemons, offers those lemons at the crossroads and go buys themselves a gin and lemonade simply because it is Tuesday. "Last resort" is just another way of saying "last drinks." Even if this is the apocalypse, that is no call to avoid making things *interesting*.

The above attitude notwithstanding, there really is no way to sugarcoat this. We *do* live in a "last resort" world. A biosphere in crisis, a wealth gap not seen since the age of empires, levels of youth unemployment that have previously triggered revolutions, total surveillance and the erosion of civil liberties, robots competing for middle class jobs that were once safe for life, an unelected overclass rigging the game at our expense, a global economy built on criminal banking and continuous war.

The balance of probability suggests that if you are not already rich, you will almost certainly never be so. Modern civilisation's fundamental promise will go unfulfilled in your lifetime. But so what? It's time for a new promise. If your deepest desire is to live the life rappers pretend to have, then you are reading the wrong book. This is a book for people who realise they can only play the hand they are dealt and *have every intention of doing so*. This is a book for people who can disassociate personal meaningfulness with generating the wealth required to achieve it. This is a book for people who realise success is individually defined and individually delivered.

It may sound surprising to bring this up as early as the introduction, but I was and remain fairly unambitious. I did a film degree in Sydney, Australia. It did not even have examinations. I am not a banker, I am not some

TV host, beaming through porcelain teeth, telling you to put your credit card in the freezer. Whisper it, but I actually find money to be a bit, well, boring. That's why this is a success magic book rather than a money magic book. The general idea is that one inevitably follows the other.

In my early twenties, my "plan A" was to be a filmmaker; if not a famous one then at least one that can pay the rent. There really was no "plan B," but I suppose it would have been some kind of retail sales if my student jobs were anything to go by. Fortunately for everyone involved—especially the cinema-going public—the universe appears to operate exclusively on "plan C." Or, at least, it certainly did and continues to do so in my case. What I will tell you is that making peace with plan C, learning to roll with and adapt to it, has turned out really quite well for me (so far!). I have lived in multiple cities on both sides of the planet, seen much of the parts in-between and worked for some of the world's largest and most-loved media companies. When one of these media companies made me redundant, as they are wont to do, I even managed to start a moderately popular chaos magic blog called *Rune Soup*, the maintenance of which has provided me with some lifelong magical friendships and led to the book you hold in your hands. Along the way I found love, a reasonable level of wealth and managed to absolutely smash through my bucket list.

Viewed over a longer timeline, what magic has always offered and what I hope to be able to impart in this book, a way to maximise plan C. Magic departs from mysticism because it proudly proclaims its unshakeable intention to do noteworthy things in this world, rather than seeking merely to transcend it. If you compare the Greek Magical Papyri of the first few centuries of the Common Era with the Neoplatonism of the same time period you see a view of the universe that is largely identical and two entirely separate ways of approaching that universe. The Greek Magical Papyri are filled with spells to end marriages, find treasure, cure livestock, banish demons, and find employment among the powerful. The magicians of the classical age lived through an era of zero social mobility and wide-ranging cultural collapse. With the assistance of the spirits, however, they were not going to let such trifling matters get in their way. One need not live permanently in this worldview but one must be willing to at least temporarily inhabit it. Graham Greene once wrote that all writers must have a splinter of ice in their hearts so that they can be involved in the world and also slightly removed, making observations. The hearts of modern magicians living through the Kali Yuga must contain glaciers.

This is where adopting a chaos magical perspective may become helpful. We have about seventy years of psychological research that demonstrates keeping a positive attitude despite the prevailing challenges is associated with eventual success or goal achievement. At this point in time it is pretty hard to argue a contrary case. Stay positive, keep your head in the game, and don't give up. We may as well pin a badge saying "full-blown science" on this statement.

To borrow a term from mathematics, such "full blown science" is "necessary but not sufficient." A cold, unblinking stare into the reality of our situation, however grim, is an essential first step, lest we run the risk of descending into fantasy and escapism. Cognitive dissonance has scuppered many magicians' ships before they have even left the harbour. It is for this reason that the opening chapter of the book you are holding is—putting it politely—*stark*. And if much of the information is new to you, then it will feel stark like a nuclear winter. I make no apologies for this. The good news, the hacks, the optimisation strategies, all follow in the subsequent chapters. If any of them strike you as particularly extreme, go back and read the first chapter again and remind yourself we are undergoing a once-in-a-civilisation economic event.

Chaos magic is not tied to a fixed model of reality or, more specifically, it need not be. It merely offers a toolkit of ideas and practices that you can use to effect change in your material circumstances. Chaos magic is largely interoperable with whatever belief system you most regularly inhabit, even if that happens to be stringent materialism. There are no mandatory interventionary divine beings, the destruction of the American middle class is not "God's will," and the last thirty years of wealth harvesting by the rich do not have anything to do with seasonal calendars or karma. You may consider chaos magic as a sort of management consultancy exercise. The book is written from a chaos magic perspective because it is probably the most useful worldview for anyone of a spiritual bent to optimise the reality of their situation given the prevailing economic headwinds. It provides us with the opportunity to examine the interplay of magic and opportunity without having to fold it back into an explanatory framework.

First and foremost, you are required to at least temporarily adopt a chaos magic headspace: Reality must be approached more from a pirate angle than a naval one. As we shall soon see, the rules of this world were simply not built for your benefit. And in an era of extreme economic change whose only corollary is the first Industrial Revolution, there are no safe harbours left, only the comparative safety of the open ocean. Your goal is not to find a quiet, secure job somewhere near an affordable suburb, settle down and then wait for death. The economy that supported such unambitious goals is ending. The developed world is now in a state of permanent structural instability. Seeking after stability is a recipe for homelessness in your late middle age years. In today's world, security only comes from embracing opportunity. And opportunity is not *randomly distributed* in either space or time. It must be pursued and seized.

Enter magic. There is a very specific bravery that comes with marshalling the forces of the universe to achieve meaningfulness and prosperity in your life. It is a bravery you must find. Magic's only other requirement is that you always put a question mark after the word "reality" and truly own the responsibility that comes with doing so.

If there is one upside to living in the Kali Yuga, it is this. According to Hindu belief, because the world has fallen so far from its original, elevated state, you need only chant Lord Krishna's name *once* to eventually achieve salvation. The gap between a person and that first mantra is greater than the gap between the second and the ten millionth mantra. Adapting this belief to a magical worldview, the gap between never having performed a practical enchantment and performing your first practical enchantment is *greater* than the gap between that first enchantment and achieving the status of Magus. Your results will also reflect the comparative size of these gaps. Fully engaging with the world as it is, on both a material and spiritual level, will quickly show you just how flimsy consensus reality actually is. One little *push* and materialism falls away like spring snow sliding off a roof. So there is an inherent paradox in using the spiritual to accomplish the material. Incorporating the magical world into your physical world will quickly show you which one is real and which one is delusion. And that realisation is more valuable than all the riches of the earth.

RECOGNIZING
THE BARS

All the totalitarian schemes add up to the same in the end, and the
approach is so insidious, the arguments so subtle and irrefutable, the
advantages so obvious, that the danger is very real, very imminent, very
difficult to bring home to the average citizen, who sees only the immediate
gain, and is hoodwinked as to the price that must be paid for it.

ALEISTER CROWLEY

We often think of economics as a dry subject of spreadsheets and interest rates but it is actually a school of philosophy. Economics is the study
of *value*. It is the study of what we consider worthwhile, where we locate
meaning on a personal and cultural level. Bad economists think it is the
study of currencies and trade imbalances, but these are only the outward
manifestations of a much, much bigger economic sphere: *what is going on*

in our heads. Probably the world's most famous transgender economist, Deirdre McClosky, prefers the term "humanomics" for this very reason.

Much of what goes on in our heads does not belong to us. It is inherited from our family and our culture. This is nowhere more evident than in economics. We inherit a system of value that is mostly unaligned to our spiritual or magical values because they come from an economy that is just simply not built for our benefit. As such, any journey toward finding meaning or value in our lives must begin with an understanding of the value system we have inherited. The mystic and science fiction author Philip K. Dick refers to this as the "black iron prison." This is his description of the worldly forces of government, economics, and culture, all largely invisible, that trap us in a small and fixed vision of reality. But the borders of our cell are arbitrary. They only imprison us if we allow them to. And so the first step in freeing yourself from prison is recognising the bars. So pour yourself a stiff drink as we go bar by bar. (Little bartender humour for you there. But seriously, pour that drink.)

Today's economic landscape is and will remain extremely unstable for a number of reasons. In the back of our minds, we all have this notion of booms and busts coming in cycles and that we just need to grit our teeth and ride through the downturn until it becomes an upturn. After that, we can go back to buying preposterously large televisions and fuel-inefficient cars. In reality, this business cycle represents only about 20 percent of the instability we currently face and about 100 percent of the government policy response to it. That alone makes things more unstable. The remaining 80 percent of the instability is down to some huge structural changes going on under the surface and away from the flapping heads you see on cable business news programmes. Some parts of the world's developed economies are permanently shrinking because they are obsolete and hugely inefficient. Other parts are expanding dramatically because of the efficiencies and cost savings they bring. This is how you end up with bankrupt, collapsed cities in one corner of the country and teenage billionaires in another. It is easier in the short term to think of them as two entirely separate economies occupying the same geographic space. It is no exaggeration to say you are living through the second Industrial Revolution.

There is an unfortunate tendency among spiritual seekers for their eyes to glaze over whenever a discussion turns to macroeconomics. A number of possibilities of why this is so present themselves. Firstly, whether as an accident of design or through the influence of actual, full-blown conspiracies that occasionally show up in history, our educational system utterly fails to impart financial literacy. If this failure remains unaddressed, we simply transfer it into our metaphysical worldview. Secondly, there is often an unexamined persistence of a Christian suspicion of the body and the physical world into an occult belief system, although this influence appears to be decreasing. Finally, learning about demons is just more *fun* than learning about consumer price inflation, even though only one of them is absolutely guaranteed to negatively affect your life. Leaving all these aside, the main reason there are so few rich wizards is most likely because they have better things to do than accrue the volumes of pointless wealth required to buy a yacht.

I understand this. At first glance, the machinations of Wall Street, various world governments, or their central banks do not appear relevant to someone whose dreams amount to having a meaningful career that provides for their family whilst leaving them enough time to pursue spiritual development. But understanding how the global financial system works does not imply you intend to scale to the very top of it, nor does it constitute any kind of endorsement. Failing to recognise that the macroeconomic is *personal* guarantees our humble, admirable dreams will go unfulfilled. Guarantees it. To suggest that these wider trends and shifts are not affecting us simply because we have no interest in learning about them is to lie to yourself and cheat yourself out of your best life.

Because this is a magic book, let us use the metaphor of astrology. When we think of personal financial literacy, we typically think of balancing the personal chequebook, managing household budgets, eliminating debt and generally being a prudent consumer. These are all essential *microeconomic* skills that we can liken to the fast-moving, smaller, frequently retrograding planets of the inner solar system. The larger, slower-moving outer planets are the *macroeconomic* forces of capital flows, commodity prices, bond markets, and equities. Both the inner and outer planets affect your chart and each other. To ignore half of them as irrelevant is to navigate with half a map, or even to divine with half a deck of tarot cards, as the macroeconomic forces will always tell you what will happen to the microeconomic forces in the coming months. Just look at how gas prices fluctuate.

To render your economic fate over to a frequently unelected power elite because you don't think you have a head for numbers is a fear response and an excuse. This provides the power elite with a strategic advantage known as *information asymmetry*. If your competitors know more than you do, they will consistently outmanoeuvre you. Upskilling our financial understanding removes this advantage. Yes, the learning curve can be steep. But if you have stepped inside a supermarket at least twice in the last five years, then you should really be more afraid of ignoring these issues than confronting them. Giving yourself a global perspective on humanomics is essential for the acquisition of wealth and meaning in your life. As the old gambling saying has it, if you can't spot the sucker at the table, *you* are the sucker.

The Dollar Under the Candle

Let us begin with a potted history of the humble dollar. Traditionally, the story of money is begun with Sumer and the Indus civilisation, but this is a deliberate obfuscation of what the dollar actually *is* today. We do not need a history of economics; we only need to find out how things got the way they are today.

From the beginning of Western civilisation right up until the end of the seventeenth century, money and wealth were more or less the same thing. You could exchange your gold and silver for other items of wealth;

cattle, property, cinnamon, other humans, and so on. If you did not exchange your gold or silver for these items then you still retained your wealth…the gold and silver in your currency. Even in a barter system, you are effectively swapping one store of wealth for another: two goats for your camel, for instance. Certainly, there was lending and credit before this date, but "wealth for wealth" was largely how money worked. The very idea that pieces of paper held value seemed alien. In fact, legendary explorer Marco Polo could not quite believe it when he encountered an early currency on his adventures. He wrote in his diary about the peculiar monetary experiment of the Great Khan:

> He makes them take of the bark of a certain tree, in fact of the
> Mulberry Tree, the leaves of which are the food of the silkworms,—
> these trees being so numerous that whole districts are full of them.
> What they take is a certain fine white bark or skin which lies between
> the wood of the tree and the thick outer bark, and this they make into
> something resembling sheets of paper, but black. When these sheets
> have been prepared they are cut up into pieces of different sizes. The
> smallest of these sizes is worth a half tornesel; the next, a little larger,
> one tornesel; one, a little larger still, is worth half a silver groat of
> Venice; another a whole groat; others yet two groats, five groats, and
> ten groats. There is also a kind worth one Bezant of gold, and others
> of three Bezants, and so up to ten. All these pieces of paper are [issued
> with as much solemnity and authority as if they were of pure gold or
> silver; and on every piece a variety of officials, whose duty it is, have
> to write their names, and to put their seals. And when all is prepared
> duly, the chief officer deputed by the Kaan smears the Seal entrusted
> to him with vermilion, and impresses it on the paper, so that the
> form of the Seal remains printed upon it in red; the Money is then
> authentic. Any one forging it would be punished with death.] And
> the Kaan causes every year to be made such a vast quantity of this

money, which costs him nothing, that it must equal in amount all the
treasure in the world.

> *With these pieces of paper, made as I have described, he causes*
> *all payments on his own account to be made; and he makes them*
> *to pass current universally over all his kingdoms and provinces and*
> *territories, and whithersoever his power and sovereignty extends.*
> *And nobody, however important he may think himself, dares to*
> *refuse them on pain of death.*[1]

Described by Marco Polo, fiat currency really does sound a bit pre-posterous, like one of those meandering thought experiments you and your buddies came up with one night while stoned in college. But a straight fiat currency is not quite the system we have today. If anything, ours is even stranger. Ours really begins toward the end of the seventeenth century, in the heart of London and in Europe's low countries.

Goldsmiths and jewellers would store deposits of their customers' wealth in their vaults and issue them receipts for the stored value. These receipts began to be swapped and traded as a more convenient method of payment than taking the receipt back to the vault, extracting your gold and paying with that. What quickly became apparent to these vault owners was that only a small fraction of depositors ever came back to extract their gold. And so for better or worse, they began issuing *more* receipts than they had gold in the vaults. The vault owners could either spend these receipts or loan them to individuals or businesses. The profits from the interest on these loans was substantial. From this point, the final step was inevitable. These vault owners could make much more from lending against these receipts than they could in charging vault fees, so they began paying people and businesses to store their wealth, which is how we ended

---

1   "The Travels of Marco Polo the Venetian." Accessed April 12, 2015.
    archive.org/details/marcopolo00polouoft.

up with interest bearing savings accounts. And so, taken together, what we know of as *fractional reserve banking* was born. You put one hundred gold coins in a vault and they hand out receipts for eight hundred gold coins. The system compounds again if these receipts are deposited in another bank who keeps only a small fraction of the receipts and lends the rest of them out, while saying they still have the initial deposit. In fact, this process of depositing and re-depositing receipts which are also lent back out accounts for more than 90 percent of all money in the global economy today. (When you take out a loan, you literally *debt* money into existence.)

It would only be a matter of time before this highly successful, legally dubious but essentially private practice was taken up by kings and governments. In the 1690s, to pay for their increasingly expensive Continental wars, the newly created—and technically privately owned—Bank of England began issuing bank notes as legal tender. These were effectively IOUs for a portion of the physical wealth stored at the bank's home on Walbrook in the city (built over the remains of an old temple to Mithras, the god of contracts).

In theory, you could front up to the Bank of England with your bank notes and exchange them for the wealth stored within. Over the next two centuries, this really was more theory than fact. Notes continued to be printed even when the gold was being spent on wars. Laws were even enacted that *prevented* the Bank from paying out gold. Where once we used to pay for things with little pieces of wealth, we began to pay for things with little pieces of *debt* in the form of IOUs. And there were a lot more IOUs than there was gold in the vault. This increased the money supply relative to the actual amount of wealth in the economy and moved control of the money supply from the market to the government. Monetary policy became intertwined with the functioning of the imperial state. Modern inflation was born.

To give credit where it is due, the central banking model was hugely successful. Britain raised a national debt, crushed her enemies and built the greatest empire the world ever knew. The policy continues to this day in the form of America's numerous oil wars. Catherine Austin Fitts, former Undersecretary of Housing and Urban Development, refers to this as "the central banking and warfare model." You invade a country and force it to accept your printed currency in exchange for its natural resources, leaving the victor with the harvested wealth as well as complete control over the value of the IOUs which are now stronger thanks to the resources you have just extracted. Since Nixon left office, the largest foreign buyers of US bonds tend to be banks in countries that we have effectively occupied militarily. Nice work if you can get it! Just as the Royal Navy did before it in India and the Caribbean, so the US military and its NATO allies do today in Eurasia.

A secondary hit on the status of money as wealth happened in the twentieth century with the complete abandonment of the gold standard. The story of the secondary hit begins in 1913 and ends in 1971. When the Federal Reserve was first created, it kept to the monetary best practice that had been so successful in Central Europe, known as the classical gold standard. If you look at dollars printed prior to the First World War, you will see it clearly written on a twenty-dollar note that it can be exchanged for twenty dollars of physical gold.

This redemption facility was suspended during the war as the "civilised" countries paid for killing people in other civilised countries by printing more and more currency. Governments also learned that they could mobilise the entire financial wealth of countries toward political ends through huge spending projects that were funded with dramatic increases in taxation. In between the wars, the classical gold standard was replaced with what was known as the gold exchange standard. In the US, that meant that the Federal Reserve could print fifty dollars for every twenty dollars of gold it had in its vaults (a 40 percent reserve ratio). Even this was not to last.

After the end of WWII, Europe was flooded with US dollars and completely out of gold. In fact, the US had two thirds of all declared gold in the world at that point, and Europe had almost none. The Bretton Woods

Agreement was quickly signed. Given that the world was already awash with dollars which were ultimately convertible into gold, it was agreed that almost every currency in the world would be backed by US dollars ... which themselves would be backed by gold. However, no reserve percentage was included in the agreement, as there had been between the wars. The Federal Reserve was free to print as many dollars as it pleased, figuring—just like those jewellers in London centuries before—that not everyone in the world would wish to cash in all their dollars for gold at the one time.

Over in France, Charles de Gaulle soon realised that there were too many dollars, or "receipts for gold stored in the US," compared to the amount of gold actually stored. So he asked for France's gold back. Almost immediately, other countries started asking for their gold back. The US lost 50 percent of its gold from 1959 to 1971. But even then, there were still twelve times the amount of dollars out there than there was gold to back it up.[2] Enter Nixon. He abandoned the gold standard and instituted the dollar standard, thus detaching every single currency in the world from any underlying relationship to physical wealth. The value of a currency became an expression of confidence in the government that issued it.

Nixon's main reason for abandoning the gold standard was due to his and his advisors' misunderstanding of the so-called balance of trade, which is whether a country exports more than it imports. Having the dollar pegged to gold meant that competing exporter countries such as Germany and Japan could lower their currency value in a way the US could not, giving them a perceived advantage. This is an unfortunate misunderstanding of American history. The reality is that trade deficits or surpluses do not really reflect much about underlying economic health. The United States has run a trade deficit for three hundred and fifty of the last four hundred years during which time it has risen to become the

---

2   James Turk and John A. Rubino. *The Money Bubble*. Wavecloud Corporation, 2014.

largest and most successful economy in history.[3] (Historically, rising trade deficits are more likely to correlate with decreasing unemployment.) People in other countries want to sell to Americans because the nation's economy is large and successful. Transactions do not take place between countries but between people. If I sell you a pencil, you are in a trade deficit to me because I have your money. But *you* now have a pencil. Go and write a best-seller. America's historic trade deficit is a reflection of the same phenomenon on a much larger scale. Steve Forbes himself, of the eponymous *Forbes* magazine, points out that a large part of the 2008 US trade deficit in China was $2.74 billion in "oil country tubular pipes."[4] This "deficit" does not reflect the feckless spending of a coddled middle class but the needs of a growing economy. So in this as in most things, Nixon was very, very wrong. There is no deficit where there is a reciprocal exchange. It is also worth pointing out that exporter countries' obsession with debasing their currencies as a way to improve exports is largely useless in improving the domestic economy. In the United States, exports account for approximately 10 percent of GDP, whereas consumption accounts for around 70 percent. Eroding consumer wealth thus probably does more harm than good. (A strong dollar reduces the international profit for multinational corporations, however, as their foreign earnings are worth *less* in US terms. I suspect this is one of the main, undeclared reasons for currency debasement.)

Until 1971, the value of the dollar was pegged to a fixed amount of precious metal just as it was at the beginning of fractional reserve banking. When the famous Voodooist Marie Laveau and her daughter were alive in the nineteenth century, a dollar was either made with a guaranteed amount

---

3   Steve Forbes and Elizabeth Ames. *Money: How the Destruction of the Dollar Threatens the Global Economy—And What We Can Do About It.* McGraw-Hill Education, 2014.

4   Ibid.

of silver, or was convertible into a specified amount. This fixed the value of a dollar into something real. So if either Laveau senior or junior had used the customary folk magical practice of putting a dollar under a candle, she would have been growing wealth from a fixed amount.

If you have tried this same piece of folk magic any time after 1971 then you are doing the opposite. In today's money, you need almost $5.78 to buy the equivalent of what a dollar could buy you in 1971. Such a magical act encodes an erosion of wealth rather than an accumulation.

The atom at the heart of your financial universe is no longer a reliable unit of wealth and it does not exist for your benefit. Savings are certainly better than no savings, but until they are converted back from IOUs into wealth, their face value is not what it appears, and this is before we even consider the rise of a global digital currency looming in the medium term. Even as the western world flirts with the possibility of mild deflation, it is worth remembering that since the creation of the Federal Reserve in 1913, the buying power of a single US dollar has declined by 95 percent.[5] It is a dodgy, imperfect indicator of what we value, but it is what we have, so we must understand it if we are to use it effectively.

The American Dream Is an Advertising Campaign

We have convinced ourselves that the brief twenty years after the war were a state of normalcy, when America was in its industrial ascendance and all its competitors lay in smoky ruins, their work forces dead on battlefields or burnt to ash in concentration camps. Unencumbered growth was there for the taking. Politicians win elections by promising a return to this world of the postwar dream state. Viewed over the lifetime of the country, however, you can see it is not the norm—it is a unique, lucky aberration. Think of it like assuming your normal life is drinking cocktails on the beach because of those two weeks you spent in Cancun a few years ago.

---

5   Forbes, ibid.

The postwar era was characterised by rapid economic growth driven by industrial expansion rather than consumption, universal employment, free education, and above all is the "holy of holies" we are told we desire: property ownership.

Let us be completely clear as to why hundreds of millions of dollars of advertising have been spent over three generations to convince us that property is a good investment: so banks can sell mortgages and governments can print GDP growth. *The End*. The rest of it, like "putting down roots" or "having an investment" is genuinely all advertising, as evidenced by your Pavlovian outrage as you read these words. Triggering an emotional attachment to mortgage debt had the beneficial side effect of anchoring an industrial workforce around a manufacturing base, and a drive through the outlying suburbs of today's Detroit should indicate how successful this was. Encouraging an ownership society was not a scam, however. Much like the Central Banking and Warfare model, it worked quite well for a couple of decades. The housing industry contributed around 20 percent to GDP through real bank profits, construction, and the creation and purchase of all the things you put in a house: fridges, couches, and so on. The fractional reserve banking system created by those goldsmiths and jewellers centuries before allowed for capital to centralise around *worthwhile* investments. Your relationship to the bank was relationship-based: the bank would assess whether you were a good investment and whether you would both make money.

As long as mortgages were kept at a ratio of between two and three times your annual salary and energy remained cheap enough to commute in from the suburbs and first time buyers made up at least 40 percent of all sales *and* as long as the economy provided the volume of stable jobs needed to support the mortgage approvals, then the whole system *working together* was very beneficial. But which part of the picture I have just painted looks like today's world?

Before we answer that, we need to pinpoint the major turning point in the system, precisely when things began to go awry. In the 1970s, the concept of securitization was introduced into the mortgage system. Simply speaking, a security is a claim on a future payment of money. So a mortgage backed security is a claim on the future payments from a bundle of hundreds or thousands of individual mortgages. Banks began selling these to other banks, pension funds, and other financial institutions. From this point, the prospective American homeowner became doubly useful. Firstly there was the GDP impact of the growing housing market. Secondly—and significantly more profitably for the financial industry—an individual mortgage was no longer seen as something a bank sold the way a baker sells bread. Individual mortgages became the "wheat" that became the flour that became the bread that gave the bank its profits. Banking moved from being relationship-based (which enabled real investment in a real economy) to being *transactional*; bankers changed from being investors to brokers.

Bundling up mortgages into financial instruments was not some conspiracy perpetrated by a cabal of cigar-smoking New Yorkers. (That came later with the bank bail-outs and the avoidance of jail time.) In the short term, "securitization" did something remarkable. It allowed poorer people to buy houses because the banks could spread these riskier mortgages in amongst lower risk ones and then make enough money off the bundle of mortgages to offer loans to more poor people. The intention was almost laudable: find a way to remove risk from offering loans to low-income customers so that more people might be able to own their own home. But what is it they say about the road to Hell and good intentions?

Pouring so much extra demand into the housing market was like pouring fuel on a fire. Prices took off, causing people to take out bigger and bigger mortgages, which made the debt/assets ever more valuable to the banks as they financialized them into derivatives and mortgage backed securities.

We went too far. By a long way. As we all know now, giving second interest-only mortgages to the permanently unemployed for houses that were already over-valued who were living in economically depressed areas broke the entire world.

By 2008, the financial instruments that had been built on these bad mortgages—and more importantly the derivatives that were constructed around them—were technically worth dozens of times more than the entire planet's economic output. When this whole monstrous zeppelin came crashing back down to earth, two things happened that nobody likes to talk about: the banks were bailed out of all their defaulted mortgages by the taxpayer, and they *also* reclaimed the houses of those who could no longer pay. It was a win-win. In the meantime, millions of Americans were forced from their homes and of those who stayed, just under half were stuck paying mortgages that were worth more than the value of their houses. Ten million jobs were lost and the banks received $11 trillion in bailouts. It is worth noting that the total mortgage debt of the United States at the time was approximately $9 trillion. It would have been cheaper for the taxpayer to pay off every single mortgage in the country and let the banks who placed dodgy bets fail. Go ahead and let that sink in.

The results of all these misdealings are plainly evident. According to the Brookings Institute, the nation's poor are now more likely to be found in the suburbs than in inner cities or regional areas.[6] With the evaporation of well-paying jobs and the increasing cost of energy—the cost of the average daily commute climbed 50 percent between 2005 and 2012—millions of Americans are now trapped in a new form of debt feudalism.[7] It is too expensive to travel for better paying jobs, and the ones available

6   Alan Berube, Elizabeth Kneebone, and Jane Williams. "Suburban Poverty Traverses Red/Blue Divide." *Brookings Research.* Accessed April 12, 2015. www .brookings.edu//media/research/files/reports/2013/08/06-suburban-poverty /suburban-poverty-by-congressional-district.pdf.

7   Jennifer Medina. "Hardship Makes a New Home in the Suburbs," *New York Times.* May 8, 2014.

locally pay considerably less than before the crash. Forty-nine million Americans are now classed as "food insecure."[8]

In today's housing market, properties that are worth more than a million dollars are selling at an increased rate of about 10 percent a year. Properties under $250,000—representing two-thirds of the total market—are declining by 12 percent year on year.[9] RealtyTrac reported that 42.7 percent of all house sales in the first quarter of 2014 were all-cash purchases...meaning no mortgage was required.[10] Reading between the lines, what we definitely are not hearing here is the sound of young couples' feet getting onto the property ladder. This is the sound of long-term investors chasing property prices to the moon where the average American cannot afford to follow. At the time of writing, first home buyer volumes have collapsed to 27-year lows, and housing's contribution to GDP is the lowest since the end of World War II.

Despite all of this manipulation, financial destruction, and ruinous amounts of personal debt, Americans continue to believe that property ownership is the best possible investment. And yet, according to the *Washington Post*, home ownership yielded only 0.3 percent per year over the last century when you remove inflation.[11] In that same period, the S&P 500 has yielded 6.5 percent per year.

Here we return to how economics is mostly about what is going on inside your head, rather than what is going on in the economy. Not only do

---

8   Hunter Stuart. "49 Million Americans Go Hungry, Despite So-Called Recovery." Accessed April 12, 2015. www.huffingtonpost.com/2014/05 /08/food-insecurity_n_5250592.html.

9   RealtyTrac Q1 2014 Foreclosure Market Report. Accessed April 12, 2015. www .realtytrac.com/content/foreclosure-market-report/q1-2014-us-institutional -investor-and-cash-sales-report-8052.

10 Ibid.

11 Catherine Rampell. "Americans Think Owning a Home Is Better for Them Than It Is." *Washington Post.* April 21, 2014.

we completely misunderstand how inflation works by failing to make the connection between the prices we pay in the supermarket and the asking price a realtor will quote us, we have been trained to *value* home ownership as an indicator of security and adulthood even though anyone on the Nobel committee will tell us otherwise. This value is arbitrary.

It is crucially important to realise that the desire for property ownership is emotional rather than strategic because in almost all areas of the country it is little more than an inflation hedge, not the supreme wealth-creating investment we wish it to be. And it is only an inflation hedge if you do not buy "too much" house and get stuck servicing too large a mortgage. When you stop and view property-mania on a long enough timeline, this all starts to make sense. Pretty much since we started building houses about ten thousand years ago, they have been multi-generational dwellings. However, in the latter half of the twentieth century, we were told we could keep three households solvent—grandparents, parents, and you—where previously we only had to keep the one solvent. The economics underpinning this gamble—and it *was* a gamble—are only becoming evident now as the third generation looks around and finds housing unaffordable.

Single-generation, owner-occupied dwellings are an eyeblink in the history of the human race, not an eternal condition. Find a better way.

Capitalism's "Bug"

It may surprise you to realise that we do not have a lot of clean data about how "normal" capitalism works. We keep having to suspend so-called true capitalism to go and fight wars, collapse empires, incorporate other genders into the work force, create fiat currencies, default on our government bonds, and rebuild entire continents. We are learning as we go along. We are not even really sure what triggered the particular brand of northern European capitalism that has been so successful in lifting billions of people out of poverty over the last two centuries, creating a global middle class. (Which isn't to say it is perfect, obviously.) The clue should have been in the name, but one of the key areas where we have limited insight is how capital—wealth in the form of money and physical assets that is available for investing—works over time. Much of this is down to our focus on credit. Credit or available debt is not inherently bad. Whilst "true capitalism" could otherwise be called "riskism" because it requires participants to put accrued capital at *risk* through investment, a functioning credit market enables current investment to be repaid with future profits. In the right scenario, this works exceptionally well.

Credit and capital are the yin and yang of capitalism. Their interplay creates the entire universe and so developing an understanding of what they are and how they work is an essential step in recognising the bars of our black iron prison. According to Deirdre McClosky, the humanomist name-checked at the beginning of the chapter, it was a culture of celebrating innovation and inventors along with the above law changes that allowed northwest Europe and its colonies to pull ahead of the rest of the world.[12] It certainly was not just available credit, which the Muslim world had been using for almost a thousand years. Nor was it technical prowess as China had been significantly more technically advanced than Europe for the previous two thousand years. Nor was it the imperial project as the Mayan, Ottoman, and Mughal empires were all better established. (Empires enrich emperors. We stay poor. Just ask Dick Cheney.) Indeed, from a functional perspective, if you looked around the globe at the end of the Dark Ages, western Europe would have been the *last* place you would have chosen for an economic and cultural transformation. McClosky's guess is as good as any. Whatever happened, it allowed personal capital to grow faster than it would through the simple re-investment of profit.

---

12   Deidre McClosky. "Measured, Unmeasured, Mismeasured and Unjustified Pessimism: A Review Essay of Thomas Piketty's *Capital in the Twenty First Century.*" *Erasmus Journal for Philosophy and Economics.* Volume 7, Issue 2. Autumn 2014.

She calls this the beginning of the Great Enrichment, the starting point of mankind's build-out of a global middle class, an event that triggered the greatest ever decentralisation and creation of wealth ever.

French economist *du jour* Thomas Piketty has studied the accumulation of capital in western countries over the last two centuries. Some surprising observations have come to light that appear to be *features* of capitalism rather than bugs. In the twentieth century it was largely hidden by the extreme re-organisation brought about by the Great Depression and World War II but in capitalist economies, capital accumulates over time in bigger and bigger amounts in smaller and smaller sets of hands. Piketty's absolute numbers have been challenged because he failed to account for wealth transfers such as government payments and housing subsidies, a huge source of wealth for the lowest income brackets. Drop them back into the metaphorical spreadsheet and much of the rate of change in wealth growth vanishes. However, the general trend of increasing wealth centralization is hard to argue against. The popular understanding of this is evidenced in the Occupy movement's promotion of the idea of the 1 percent, a notion owing no small part to Piketty's previous research.

Whilst it is true that literally all of the economic gains since the 2008 crash have gone to the top 10 percent and most of this has gone to the top 1 percent, even these vanishingly small numbers of people hide quite how centralised global capital has become. Yes, the top 10 percent take home 50 percent of the country's income … indeed it is the only part of the economy whose income growth has exceeded inflation over the last four decades. But measuring the 1/99 percents on *income* rather than *capital* —that is, money *earned* rather than wealth *owned*—is what everybody but Thomas Piketty missed. The numbers look less catchy on a placard, but the real concern is the 0.1 percent. Thanks to the erosion of incomes for the vast majority, the 1 percent now includes doctors and even some university professors, neither of whom you are likely to see splashing out on private jets.

The general assumption about capital was that it is re-invested into the real economy, for example, in the form of industrialists building new factories which create additional jobs and have service sectors spring up around them. Capital growth was best achieved through judicious capital expenditure. This certainly happened and still happens. However Piketty has observed a general trend for the increasing centralization of capital in fewer and fewer hands, leading to a disastrous scenario where a few dozen people can effectively buy the entire political process, and do so with an amount of wealth so small to them it would be akin to what you or I find between the couch cushions. According to Oxfam, in 2012 alone, the top hundred richest people on earth earned enough money to end world poverty four times over.[13]

It has only been in the last few years that we have even been able to visualise just how small such a group of people actually is. Regarding the most recent financial crisis, much of the vitriol has been directed at the banks as the cause of the meltdown. This is blaming the handgun rather than the gunman. Over the last three generations we have seen a huge shift in business and capital ownerships from independent operators into a centralised, transnational world. You only need to stroll down your main street to see this.

The real story in the centralisation of wealth and power is in who owns the banks and the world's largest corporations. These are called institutional investors and they include pension funds and other private pools of capital. They are the leviathans in the financial ocean and their movements trigger king tides. The largest thirty institutional shareholders of the top 299 corporations on earth own 51.4 percent of all shares. Of

---

13 "The Cost of Inequality: How Wealth and Income Extremes Hurt Us All." Oxfam Report, January 18, 2013. www.oxfam.org/sites/www.oxfam.org/files/cost-of -inequality-oxfam-mb180113.pdf.

these thirty, only nine are sovereign governments or their wealth funds.[14] In recent years, some complex system theorists working out of the Swiss Federal Institute of Technology in Zurich have calculated that 40 percent of the wealth in the global capitalist network is controlled by less than one percent of the companies within that same network; a super-entity of 147 corporations with interlocking boards of directors.[15] Most of these were financial institutions and the top twenty included Barclays Bank, JP Morgan Chase, and Goldman Sachs.

The futility of protesting Bilderberg meetings or Bohemian Grove quickly becomes evident when you realise that trillions of dollars can be moved into and out of markets as a result of a single conference call of up to ten people. And that is more or less exactly what happens. Centralised capital can move very fast.

This situation sets up a peculiar imbalance in incentives which favours the hugely wealthy at our expense. Firstly, there is the impact on tax revenue which has to be made up in what is left of the real economy. Half of all global trade now passes through tax havens and an estimated one third of the world's wealth resides there permanently. In the mean time, you and I are left to pay for the roads and the schools from the declining income we make in an economy that has been drained of almost all capital investment now that it has been put to good use in Taiwan and Brazil.

These incentives become even more bizarre when you consider pension funds, some of the largest institutional investors. Think on this. You spend your entire career paying money that you earned in America or Britain's real economy into a pot that is then taken out of the country and invested in an emerging market ... with the result that it destroys jobs

---

14   Andy Coghlan and Deborah MacKenzie. "Revealed—The Capitalist Network That Runs the World." *New Scientist.* October 22, 2011.

15   Ibid.

in the economy you worked in, making everyone poorer and increasing your tax obligation as more people have to rely on social programmes.

And why is this money taken out of the country? Because you want your pension fund to have the highest return on investment so that you can actually retire one day in a corner of the world that is now economically depressed as a result of this pooling of capital you contributed to your whole life. So do you want the companies your pension fund invested in paying more or less tax? If they pay less tax, you have a bigger pension, but you pay more for roads. Whether you call this a conspiracy or "just good business" is irrelevant because not only is it happening, but it sets the agenda for how you generate your own wealth. Because make no mistake, your pension fund currently cannot afford to pay out what it has promised you. To use a small change analogy, the baby boomers' pension payout is a claim of one dollar a year on only fifteen cents in savings.

It thus emerges that capitalism itself is not the problem. Far from it. Capitalism triggered the Great Enrichment and will go on to lift billions more out of poverty in developing countries in the coming five decades. It does however have a bug, and that bug's name is *centralization.* Everyone is getting richer, but some people are getting rich faster than others. This process would be none of our business if it did not have huge political implications, which sadly it does. The board on which we hope to play the game of Life is set up and packed up based on which corner of the world promises the best return on capital for a few dozen unbelievably wealthy people. Actually being aware of this provides you with a strategic advantage in wealth generation and also in providing personal meaning. Pagans typically focus on preventing ecological debasement as a core spiritual activity, but the movement of capital is at the very heart of all this. Your pension funds are investing in energy companies that are burning down the Amazon so that they can pay you to retire in a corner of America that is being destroyed by fracking—depressing house prices and ruining your local ecosystem—

because that very same capital was not invested in local green energy infrastructure like wind or solar power down the road from you.

Debasement

For most people living in the West, incomes have not grown in real terms for the last forty years. How is it then that an average income forty years ago could support an entire family, two cars, and property ownership? The answer is for the same reason that everyone thinks their houses have increased in value when they haven't: inflation. I recall reading Archie comics as a child and marvelling at the cost Jughead would pay for his hamburgers ... twenty-five cents! And a milkshake for a dime. Good luck finding a hamburger for twenty-five cents in an independent diner today. (And good luck finding an independent diner today.)

It is a common misconception that inflation means prices going up. This is not so. Inflation, to borrow the definition from the Austrian School, is an increase in the money supply. Higher prices are just one potential result and a result that is typically unevenly distributed. Increasing money does not flow evenly into the real economy but instead inflates particular assets ... such as housing in the 2000s or dot-com companies in the 1990s. (Or it just sits as reserves in big banks, reducing the velocity and actually triggering deflation instead.) The dual effect of this increasing money supply is an erosion in normal savings/earning potential for middle economies and an increase in the value of assets those same people cannot typically afford, such as equities and investment properties. This means that the gap between the rich and poor actually gets wider as a side effect of the "normal" monetary policy that is supposed to be designed to boost the entire economy. This is why I will use the word debasement rather than inflation, because it more accurately captures the systemic impact of monetary policy on your life. The most important wealth creation step you can ever take is to come to grips with debasement and find ways to ameliorate it.

How did we get into this situation in the first place? With the currencies of the world no longer fixed to a finite commodity—gold or silver—we create new money simply by printing it. (More accurately, someone enters a few more zeroes into a spreadsheet somewhere.) Putting aside the Federal Reserve's constitutionally dubious status as a private bank, it is important to realise that its primary purpose is to fund the government. Briefly, the Treasury works out how much money it needs to pay for the government's various projects and then sells bonds to banks to cover this amount. Now the Treasury has the money the government needs and the banks have these bonds. So the banks take these bonds and sell them to the Federal Reserve. It is this act of a private bank selling a government document to the Federal Reserve that creates money. The Fed magics up the amount needed to buy the bonds from the banks, hey presto, money exists... and the banks have it. The Fed can also push the interest rates down further by purchasing bonds directly, which it has done in the past.

A bond is a promise to pay back a loan of money plus a certain amount more at the end of an agreed term. But it is not like a loan that an individual may take out which requires some form of asset to borrow against. The government in question simply promises to pay the money back. This is why the international market uses bond sales and yields as a measure of confidence in a particular country's economy or governance. If the market is uncertain about the government, the government in question drops the price of bonds and promises to pay back substantially more at the end of the term, which drives up the bond yield.

Having the largest pool of potential buyers is a good thing for a government because the increase in demand means you don't have to promise to pay back quite so much. As a result, some fairly dubious policy decisions end up being implemented, such as laws being passed that classed government bonds as 100 percent "safe assets." This incentivised large financial institutions to hold more of them as part of their minimum capital requirements needed to lend against. Yes, you read that right, banks can issue loans against government loans and call them assets. Like so many of the policies in this chapter, running a government debt based on money that is invented out of thin air worked quite well for a while. With a growing tax base from a low-unemployment, productive economy, it is a very good way to rapidly invest in infrastructure, education, and healthcare to further grow the productive economy which further grows your tax base. Inevitably, things went awry. People got elected on expensive promises, black budget spending grew, great chunks of the productive economy were offshored to developing markets… all of which reduced the tax base and increased government obligations through welfare and warfare.

When these government promises (bonds) were due, it became easier at first to pay these out by issuing more promises rather than paying out of the tax haul. Then it became essential. Government debt ballooned.

Where government debt actually *is* like private debt is in the servicing of interest payments. When you borrow money, some portion of your income needs to be allocated to paying interest on your debt. We all know this from personal experience. The more you borrow, the larger the amount of your income needs to go to paying interest. If your income—or tax haul—does not grow faster than your interest payments, you have a very big problem.

Do you know the fastest way to get out of debt when you control the money supply? Debasement. Printing more money—reducing the buying power of the dollar—allows someone to pay today's debt in tomorrow's reduced currency. If you borrow $100 today and spend it but that $100 is only worth $80 in three years, you are winning. When you combine this with keeping interest rates low you end up with what many people now call financial repression; which is keeping interest rates below the rate of inflation so governments can "inflate away" their debt. In the meantime, this exact same process erodes personal savings as they are worth less in the future. The money we are talking about is far from chump change.

According to the 150-year-old Swiss insurer, Swiss Re, American savers have lost $470 billion in interest income since the 2008 financial crisis.[16]

Debasing the currency has other economic effects that benefit people who are not you or me. We are told that a weak dollar is important for export growth, but exports only account for around 10 percent of US GDP. A weak dollar allows for companies to inflate the value of their international profits which boosts stock prices. In fact, gradually debasing the value of the dollar means that stock prices and other assets appear more valuable without any underlying business improvement due simply to the Jughead hamburger effect. When you consider the fact that the bottom 90 percent of Americans own less than 20 percent of all stocks and mutual funds, it is quite clear who this policy helps the most and who it hurts the most.

The effect of these policies on the average person has been deliberately masked over the last twenty years. Have you ever had the experience of watching a news programme tell you that inflation is too low and trying to reconcile that with your experience at the grocery store? Well, you are right and they are lying. Since its inception right up until the early 1990s, the Consumer Price Index (CPI) measured the cost of living by checking the prices of an *identical* basket of goods over time, a practice dating back to the 1700s. However, in the second half of the twentieth century, academia became concerned that the measurement was inaccurate because it did not track consumer substitution for cheaper goods when one became more expensive such as swapping steak for chicken. As such, inflation may be overstated in what was measured and would lead to interest rate changes that may be unnecessary.

Nothing was really done about this until the early 1990s when policy makers "suddenly" became concerned that the CPI was "inaccurate"

16   "Financial Repression: The Unintended Consequences." Published March 28, 2015. www.swissre.com/media/news_releases/nr_20150326_financial _repression.html.

because it did not allow substitution. Thanks largely to the efforts of Newt Gingrich and Alan Greenspan, the CPI began to be calculated with a marvellously technocratic term: "hedonic quality adjustment." In real terms, this not only allowed for a substitution of steak for chicken, it allowed for buying less chicken, it assumed bulk-purchases of perishable items from discount outlets, and it changed the weight of foodstuffs. Essentially, it completely broke a two-hundred-year-old way of measuring the cost of living by allowing policy makers to gerrymander the rate of inflation to whatever they needed it to be.

Why would anyone want to do this? Well, you will recall that it was in the 1990s that Greenspan poured vast amounts of cheap credit into the economy to inflate both a housing bubble and a tech bubble. You can only accomplish this by fully detaching your setting of interest rates from the real economy. The secondary reason is even more insidious and was of particular interest to Gingrich. Pretending inflation was low allowed policy makers to claim that on-paper wage increases—which were a result of their own dollar printing—were "real." This inflated more households into higher tax brackets and reduced Social Security payments as everyone was now "richer."

Let us put this all together. Policy is set based on the belief that you can technically swap out genetically modified chicken for dog food to feed your children in order to balance out continuous money printing and this means you are getting richer so you now pay more tax and receive less government support. But just have a look at the S&P 500, eh?

Bringing it up to the present day, those spurious wage increases are not even happening. Median household income is down 7 percent since 2000. It is down substantially more when you strip the top 10 percent of households out of that number. In fact, the majority of Americans are now 40 percent poorer today than they were in 2007. According to Gabriel Zucman at UC Berkeley, almost half of Americans have *zero* wealth (their debts equal or exceed their assets). In the meantime, the top 16,000 families have 12 percent of it.[17]

Catherine Austin Fitts, former Undersecretary of Housing and Urban Development, regularly uses her tuna fish example to illustrate the effect of all this: each year a can of tuna costs 10 percent more, has 10 percent less tuna in it, and is 10 percent more likely to make you sick. Debasement in a can.

Demographics

Today, ten thousand Americans will retire. The same thing will happen tomorrow. The same thing will happen the next day and every day after that until the year 2030. The departure of the baby boomers from the workforce is a demographic event unprecedented in the history of mankind.

Congratulations to them. Congratulations and good luck because there are currently trillions and trillions in unfunded pension liabilities in both public and private plans. You will recall that the bank bailouts amounted to a "mere" $13 trillion. The combined public and private pension liabilities are difficult to calculate but sit between $80 and $90 trillion. Those are some big promises. This is before we get to the dramatic increase in healthcare costs associated with a doubling of the number of senior citizens in the developed economies of the world in the next three decades.

It is not really their fault, but the baby boomers are the economic equivalent of a biblical locust swarm. When they were born, there was a huge growth in diapers and prams. They received largely free healthcare and education which prepared them for the abundance of middle class jobs that were available in a successful economy. They benefitted from effectively free housing as properties inflated along their entire working lives.

---

17   Noel King. "About half of America has zero net wealth." Accessed April 12, 2015. www.marketplace.org/topics/wealth-poverty/about-half-america-has-zero-net -wealth.

The impact of their presence in tertiary education and the property market made both considerably more expensive which led to funding cuts for the generations that came after them. (Heaven forbid the taxes from the jobs they received by virtue of their free education should be paid back into the college system.)

The story of the western consumer economy is really the story of the things baby boomers buy. We actually know quite a bit about the life cycle of a consumer now. People buy houses at around the same age, 31. People buy international vacations in their forties. People buy luxury cars at around the age of 53 once the kids have graduated college and before the drivers get too old to enjoy them. The peak age for potato crisp purchase is 42 years old, by the way.[18] So this is quite granular information.

What do retirees buy? Pretty much nothing. Whilst it may initially look like a good news employment story that the baby boomers are vacating well-paying middle-class jobs, what this actually means is that the biggest source of demand in an economy that is 70 percent based on consumption is evaporating, which obviously puts the jobs they are vacating at risk. This means the consumer economy is shrinking just at the time when we need it to be about twenty times larger to pay for the increased social welfare and healthcare costs associated with having a dramatic increase in senior citizens. We know household consumption peaks when its head is 46 years old. For the boomers, this happened in 2007. On a demographic basis, the consumer economies of North America and Western Europe are shrinking.

Sixty percent of Americans say they have less than $25,000 saved for retirement and 56 percent of retirees are still in debt when they retire.[19] As we saw a few pages back, this demographic inevitability has led and will

---

18   Kyle Smith. "Aging America heading for disaster." *New York Post.* February 8, 2014.

19   Michael Snyder. "22 Facts About the Coming Demographic Tsunami That Could Destroy Our Economy All by Itself ." Accessed April 12, 2015. www .theeconomiccollapseblog.com/archives/22-facts-about-the-coming -demographic-tsunami-that-could-destroy-our-economyall-by-itself.

continue to lead to erratic behaviour by the pension funds, some of the biggest sources of money on the planet. What would you do if you were a pension fund manager and you know you only have about 10 percent of the capital you need to fund your obligations? You would slosh your money around the planet looking for the highest possible yield opportunities because you do not have the time or the risk appetite to invest in the productive economy. Many of the highest yield opportunities have been in emerging markets, meaning the investments made by US pension funds do not tend to be associated with a high growth in well-paying domestic jobs.

Combined with debasement, the sloshing around of these truly enormous sums of money into new technologies will be the defining economic stories of the next ten years. It is in the demographics that we see most clearly the old economy which is going away and the new economy which is emerging.

It may not look like it to us right now, but this new economy is actually much, much bigger than the old. The story of the middle class in Europe and America is one of decline, but the middle class is growing rapidly on a planetary basis. Our decline is part of a wider rebalancing where once we were the only game in town and could consume all the resources and opportunities. Now we are moving into a world where competition for resources and opportunities is truly global.

Demography is destiny. Demography and robotics.

Following the Robot Herds

Humans have a number of important cognitive blind spots when it comes to assessing economic risk. The first is the assumption that tomorrow is going to be more or less like today. The second is a limited ability to think in terms of exponentiation. We use the word "exponential" all the time, but we use it incorrectly as a synonym for "more." A duck can count her ducklings. A monkey can become visibly upset if another monkey receives more food than him. We can process numbers and we can process more versus less. Exponentiation eludes us because we typically only encounter it in algal blooms or cancer cells.

An example of this bias in action comes from Brynjolfsson and McAfee's highly recommended book, *The Second Machine Age*.[20] The game of chess was invented in the sixth century in the Gupta empire. So impressed was the emperor with the wise man who invented it that he asked him to name his reward. The wise man asked only for some rice to feed his family but suggested they use the chessboard to determine how much. A single grain of rice placed on the first square, two grains of rice on the next, four on the next, eight on the next and so on. Halfway through the board, the wise man is up to about four billion grains of rice—about one rice paddy—and the emperor suddenly realises to what he has consented. Filling the second half of the chessboard would require eighteen quintillion grains of rice, more than has ever been farmed before. The pile of it would be so large, it would dwarf Mount Everest. As is typically the case when you tangle with the elite, the emperor kept the rice and the wise man lost his head.

In terms of the impact of automation on the developed economy we are halfway through the chessboard. We have arrived at the inflection point where the technology is already in place and has already largely destroyed well-paying working class jobs. In 20 percent of today's American families, everyone is unemployed.[21] The second half of the chessboard is where the middle class jobs are, and the robots are coming for them now.

There is a tendency to assume that automation only affects repetitive tasks such as factory processes, but robots are already being used in some European care homes. You only need to look at your smartphone to realise this is a very limited understanding of technology and innovation. Science fiction has already become science reality. Professions such as accountancy,

20   Erik Brynjolfsson and Andrew McAfee. *The Second Machine Age: Work, Progress, and Prosperity in a Time of Brilliant Technologies*. W. W. Norton & Company, 2014.

21   "Employment Characteristics of Families—2013." Bureau of Labor Statistics. Accessed April 12, 2015. www.bls.gov/news.release/pdf/famee.pdf.

law, and medicine—anywhere that relies on an expert understanding of a largely fixed body of knowledge—are at risk. Most medical diagnostic functions will be fulfilled by technology instead of people; eventually your own home will diagnose you. Think of what a robot toilet could learn about your health before emailing over-the-counter treatment suggestions before you even know you are unwell. (And think of how profitable a company that can engineer billions of dollars of cost out of the healthcare system would be. *Then* think of how much wealthier you would be if you invested in *it* rather than a mortgage. Welcome to the future.)

It is perhaps not very obvious to us because we value "expertise," but the majority of the work performed by doctors, lawyers, and accountants is largely rote. Would you pay ten dollars for an accountancy AI to be let loose on all your financial information, or would you continue to pay a hundred dollars an hour for a human accountant? The economic implications of this become clear when you realise that an accountancy AI does not need to buy a house, vacation, or even a coffee. And the unemployed accountant will not be able to afford one.

At the other end of the scale you have truck drivers and taxi drivers who will be imminently replaced with driverless cars and drones. Automation will impact the entire spectrum. According to Oxford University, financial account managers, local government administrators, retail bank employees, and NGO officers are 95 percent likely to be automated in the next decade. Over a third of all British jobs may well be automated by 2030.[22]

Looking at that list of at-risk jobs, the most important factor they all share is that they come from sectors whose principal cost is wages. This is especially the case for government and NGO roles. Returning to the example of the robot toilet and its role in the US healthcare industry. Healthcare

---

22 Carl Benedikt Frey and Michael A. Osborne. "The Future of Employment: How Susceptible Are Jobs to Computerisation?" September 17, 2013. www.futuretech .ox.ac.uk/sites/futuretech.ox.ac.uk/files/The_Future_of_Employment_OMS _Working_Paper_1.pdf.

currently consumes 20 percent of GDP and this percentage is rising as the population ages. Forty percent of healthcare costs are administrative rather than frontline; making and reviewing insurance claims, etc. Just streamlining the payment system alone will save billions. It will also permanently remove hundreds of thousands of middle class jobs from the economy.

It is so important to understand that the primary cost in the service sector is labour. You may think it is just your salary, but it is also your healthcare and retirement obligations that add another half onto what you cost your employer. In manufacturing, the largest cost *used* to be labour. Manufactured goods have reduced in price by about half by reducing this cost by the same amount. (Now energy is the principal cost in manufacturing, and even that is coming down due to the massive investment in shale and fracking—for better or for worse—as well as the manipulation of the global energy market so as to hurt America's alleged enemies.) In the service sector, if you want to reduce your costs by half, the only thing to cut is labour. Historically, we can say that such a compelling opportunity for margin growth will not go ignored for long.

The suggestion that technology permanently removes jobs from an economy rather than just shifts them is usually called the Luddite fallacy. As you can probably tell from its name, it is not popular with economists. Or, at least, with economists who can't count or prefer to focus on the first half of the chessboard. As computer science pioneer Jaron Lanier points out in *Who Owns The Future*, when Kodak was at the height of its power it had a market capitalisation of $28 billion and employed 140,000 people, all of whom could afford cars and housing and families and so on. When Instagram was sold to Facebook for a billion dollars, it had thirteen employees and had not made a single cent in revenue.[23]

---

23 Scott Timberg. "Jaron Lanier: The Internet destroyed the middle class." Accessed April 12, 2015. www.salon.com/2013/05/12/jaron_lanier_the _internet_destroyed_the_middle_class.

Yes, there will always be dentists and nurses. There will just be one of them where there used to be one hundred. We tend to fixate on the impact of technology on the technological sector, such as the replacement of personal computers with smart phones as the principal means of accessing the web. But the same technological change is transforming every sector of the economy. During the nineteenth century, as Charles Hugh Smith points out, approximately half the workforce was employed in agriculture.[24] Now that is around 2 percent. At the beginning of the twentieth century, the largest employment sector was domestic help, which should tell you everything about the effect of automation.

Hidden in those data about the collapse of agricultural employment and the rise of domestic service is a trend that is declining today: willingness to relocate for economic reasons. Specifically in these numbers you see the effect of urbanisation as people move into the cities looking for work. Today in the west, we seem to have confused comfort for happiness, but our ancestors were not so stupid. Historically, Americans under the age of 35 were twice as likely to move as those over it. According to the Brookings Institute, 31 percent did so in 1965, during the peak of American economic dominance. Today, with fewer jobs and more graduates, only 20 percent have done so.[25] A willingness to move—a taste for adventure—is itself a large strategic advantage.

Conclusion

So those are the bars. How is that drink looking? What we are witnessing is not simply the after-effects of a severe recession. We are living through some permanent structural changes to the old industrial economy as

---

24   Charles Hugh-Smith. *Get a Job, Build a Real Career and Defy a Bewildering Economy*. CreateSpace, 2014.

25   William H. Frey. "Millennial and Senior Migrants Follow Different Post-Recession Paths." Brookings Research. Accessed April 12, 2015. www.brookings.edu/research /opinions/2013/11/15-millennial-senior-post-recession-frey.

another hyper-growth economy emerges and occupies the same geographic area, by which I mean the whole planet. Meanwhile, the world's biggest workforce is heading out of the consumer economy and into retirement while the rise of automation and new technology appear to drastically alter the working lives of the generations coming up behind. These generations will have to compete for access and opportunity with the emergence of a global, connected, educated middle class. Oh yes, all of this is happening against a backdrop of environmental degradation and an increased risk of war.

We are off the map here. If someone tries to tell you otherwise, or that economic and financial policy is too complicated for you to possibly understand, that person is attempting to rob you. I know it does not sound like it, but the good news is that *no one knows what is going on.*

When a currency is manipulated as dramatically as the US dollar is manipulated—and it is the lot of a global reserve currency to be used in such a way—it breaks its ability to accurately measure price. "Price" is how *valuable* a product or service is to *you.* We live in a world where the number of inches in a foot and the distance each inch measures are constantly changing to suit the needs of the 0.01 percent. It thus falls to you and you alone to assess value, something you cannot do without an understanding of currency and money.

These are the macro forces swirling around your own individual quest for your best life. They affect everything from which side of the earth you choose to live on to the price you are willing to pay for farmers' market jam actually made by humans. It is important to realise that those we have elected to deal with these challenges are all reliant on economic policies from the nineteenth century or before. Capitalism, liberalism, Marxism, and socialism all emerged in a time when we did not even have cars, let alone space robots on other planets. The final policy, Keynesianism, originated in the 1930s. The way we view economics then, the way we measure and allocate value, is the very definition of bringing a knife to a gunfight. It is simply not up to the challenges or opportunities the twenty-first century presents. You alone have to meet those challenges and opportunities.

All these changes are going to elevate many people and are going to leave even more behind. And if you are expecting some form of policy change to save you, then you will be waiting a long time. According to a Princeton study published in early 2014, the wishes of the average American have precisely zero impact on government policy.[26] And each day you wait for a politician to save you brings you one day closer to an unfunded retirement.

There is no avoiding the fact that we are now solely responsible for our own economic destiny. Taking the long view of history, we always were, but this has been obscured by the fact that for a brief thirty-year period after the war, our economic best interest was aligned with that of the state. Now it isn't. Now we have to educate ourselves and become whole.

The first step in educating ourselves is to see through what the late, lamented, rogue political theorist Joe Bageant called "the American hologram."

All Americans, regardless of caste, live in a culture woven of self-referential illusions... A simulated republic of eagles and big box stores, a good place to live so long as we never stray outside the hologram.[27]

The good thing about holograms, of course, is that they are by definition illusory. You do not need to choose them for your maps. You can find a better map. And if you can map the world, you can probably run it.

---

26   Martin Gilens, and Benjamin I. Page. "Testing Theories of American Politics: Elites, Interest Groups, and Average Citizens." Accessed April 12, 2015. journals .cambridge.org/action/displayAbstract?fromPage=online&aid=9354310.
27   Joe Bageant. "The Great American Media Mind Warp." Accessed April 12, 2015. www.joebageant.com/joe/2007/08/the-great-ameri.html.

A PROBABILISTIC UNIVERSE

When you develop your opinions on the basis of weak evidence, you will have difficulty interpreting subsequent information that contradicts these opinions, even if this new information is obviously more accurate.

NASSIM NICHOLAS TALEB

Success is a head game. More specifically, it is a head game of *chance* rather than one of skill or strength. If there is good news in the grim story of the previous chapter, it is that the entire system is a human construct, an overlay on a probabilistic universe. It is flimsy, a hologram inside another hologram. The most insidious way the holographic bars trap you is by convincing you of their eternal, physical reality.

One of the most practicable ways of breaking out of these bars is through a diligent exploration of consciousness and probability. Marching in lockstep with a centralised, extractive late capitalist economic system is the religious faith known as scientific materialism. If only the physical exists, then only the physical has importance. If you are just a bag of chemicals, if your brain is the same thing as your mind, if you are simply a meat robot, then despite the lived personal experience of every human who has ever existed indicating the complete contrary, the worth and value of your life can be precisely measured in physical terms based on the objects you manage to accrue around you.

The hypothesis of materialism is extremely weak. A single example of the non-physical in action, be it telepathy or psi effects, a religious miracle of any flavour, a provable example of divination or precognition, and Richard Dawkins's house of dreary cards comes crashing down. There are thousands and thousands of examples to choose from and you are well-served collecting those that are most personally meaningful to you over the course of your lifetime. It could be the otherwise-impossible past life recollections of children, it could be the 120 years of university studies into telepathy and other psi results. Find something that *simply cannot be but is* and get really knowledgeable about it. These data points become talismans to ward off the demon hosts of the materialist tyranny.

The inherent weakness of the materialist hypothesis neatly explains why the scientific establishment remains wilfully, deliberately ignorant of and vigorously opposed to fields such as parapsychology. Inviting it into the canon of approved knowledge, even just as the unloved ginger stepchild of psychology (which it isn't), breaks the rest of the college. In the words of notorious British metaphysician David Icke "they defend the first domino." The magician must flick and flick until it tumbles.

At times of economic transition, old maps no longer navigate through unfamiliar streets. Chaos magic helps here. If you believe, as I do, that it is more or less mandatory for magicians to have adventures, then we can extend the metaphor by suggesting that a well-prepared adventurer always travels with more than one map. There may indeed be a resting worldview you prefer for the quieter moments in life or their most important milestones such as births, romance, and the deaths of loved ones and enemies. These maps may not be best suited for navigating the corporate sphere, especially now that it appears to have gone completely feral. (Who is the Egyptian goddess of high frequency trading, for instance? Who is the saint of downsized workers? What is the herbal charm against having your job automated?)

In order to navigate a wealth creation system that is not built for our benefit, the most appropriate maps are offensive rather than defensive. Poking holes in the dominant narrative robs it of much of the unconscious power it holds over you. Visits with the bank manager suddenly generate significantly less anxiety when their absurdity is laid bare. They emerge as a meeting of holograms to discuss things that have no objective reality in a probabilistic universe filled with chaotic high strangeness. Honestly, it's like a surrealist theatre piece when you stop to think about it.

There is, however, a danger in building out an adventurer's map that must chart the advantages and shortcomings of science. The magician may find him- or herself accidentally believing that the map is in some sense true. All too often people seek to "prove" this or that mystical worldview by recourse to scientific findings. This is a fool's errand, as mysticism is fundamentally irrational and that is its great power and solace. "Proving" mysticism with science is like using a slide-rule to measure wind speed.

In either case, in all cases, the best we can ever say is that some maps overlap more than others, which may be useful in navigating a particular metaphoric mountain range or mangrove swamp. Neither map actually is the mountains or the swamp, and neither map is particularly useful on the open ocean. I am not selling and will never sell you a worldview. I merely want to help you find the spot marked X.

Quantum Abuse

The spiritual and occult worlds subject themselves to two different versions of what I refer to as quantum abuse. The first is to slap the word "quantum" in front of some recycled New Thought claptrap and start running classes above a local bookshop. This form of abuse bothers me the least as the inexorability of market forces tends to run such groups out of town fairly quickly.

It is the second form of quantum abuse I find the most troubling. At the moment it is apparently fashionable to declare that quantum mechanics don't really tell us anything about magic or that its influence has been overstated. This is intellectually lazy (not to mention highly inaccurate), and it emanates most often from the corners of the field that intend to stick doggedly to whatever religious explanation of the universe they prefer. As famous twentieth-century physicist Niels Bohr once remarked, "If a person does not feel shocked when he first encounters quantum theory, he has not understood a word of it." Because quantum theory *does* tell us something important about magic, something that may be hugely important. It tells us that, at least in some situations, probability—or the nonphysical—has an *objective* status. It may be something that is real with a capital R.

A hybrid form of quantum abuse is to rely on theories of quantum mechanics that are approaching almost a century old or to unthinkingly cleave to the least likely interpretation of experimental results. The most egregious example of this is the metaphysical community's attachment to the many worlds hypothesis. Let us be clear as to what the hypothesis actually is: a mathematical fudge currently being used to cling to scientific materialism in the face of quantum indeterminacy results. As you are probably aware from high school science classes, an electron exists in a state of probability everywhere in its probability field surrounding the nucleus. It is only when we seek to measure it that it collapses down to a single location. These are the experimental *results* the many worlds hypothesis seeks to explain.

This explanation relies on the completely untestable hypothesis that each time a measurement of the electron happens, our entire universe actually splits into two (or however many universes are required to satisfy the possible locations of the electron). It sounds nice and magical, maybe even a little bit sciency, but it is both bad magic and bad science. What the many worlds hypothesis is saying is that probability definitely does *not* have an objective existence. Quantum nonlocality does not really exist and that *all* possible locations for the electron are occurring simultaneously in other dimensions... this means that scientific materialism is still "true" and the only things that exist are physical. It is just that all these other physical things now exist in an infinite number of dimensions that we cannot contact or ever prove exist. My little nephew has an imaginary friend who exhibits many similar properties. The whole thing is highly convenient and, frankly, highly religious. But "religious" is probably the best descriptor for materialism, anyway. As the philosopher Thomas Nagel remarks, "materialism is a premise of science, not a finding."[28]

For the purposes of achieving our best lives, we are not really in the market for *explanations* of how quantum mechanics may really work. We are merely looking for observations of scientific data that lead either to greater ideological freedom or to improved magical results. Chaos magic is as single-minded as a locust swarm in this regard. You are free to fold back whatever results you find into your wider spiritual worldview.

The aggregate observation of the last century of quantum research begins to paint a picture that is both very old and very new. We begin to see the—dare we say it—*provability* of not only the existence of consciousness but also its primacy. If the implications that consciousness is the fundamental stuff of the universe sounds Vedic, there is probably a good reason for that. Most of the founding fathers of quantum theory were dedicated

---

28   John Horgan. "Is scientific materialism almost certainly false?" *Scientific American.* January 30, 2013. blogs.scientificamerican.com/cross -check/2013/01/30/is-scientific-materialism-almost-certainly-false/.

Vedantists. Heisenberg himself stated that "quantum theory will not look ridiculous to those who have read Vedanta."[29] As for Max Planck:

I regard consciousness as fundamental. I regard matter as derivative from consciousness. Everything that we talk about, everything that we regard as existing, postulates consciousness.[30]

Observer effects suggest a fundamental interrelationship between consciousness and matter which is called in quantum panpsychism chaos magic. From *The Octavo* by Peter J. Carroll, chaos magic's founder:

Quantum panpsychism suggests that we turn the whole argument on its head and interpret parapsychological events as evidence for the absence of spirit or mind as phenomena separate to matter.

Miraculous, parapsychological, magical events tend to occur rather capriciously and infrequently on the macroscopic scale. However on the quantum scale they occur frequently and in a much more dependable fashion. The quantum level of reality seethes with weirdness, quanta appear to teleport by disappearing at one place and appearing at another, they appear to communicate instantaneously across space and probably time as well, sometimes they appear to exist in two places simultaneously, or in two contradictory states at the same time, and they may travel backwards in time.[31]

---

29 David Storoy. "Did the Vedic Philosophy Influence the Concept of Free Energy and Quantum Mechanics?" *Science and Nonduality*. Accessed April 12, 2015. www.scienceandnonduality.com/did-the-vedic-philosophy-influenced-the -concept-of-free-energy-and-quantum-mechanics/.

30 Quoted in *The Observer* (25 January 1931). Cited in Joseph H. Fussell, "Where is Science Going?: Review and Comment," *Theosophical Path Magazine*, January to December 1933 (2003), 199.

31 Peter J. Carroll. *The Octavo: A Sorcerer-Scientist's Grimoire*. Mandrake of Oxford, 2010.

The influence of consciousness at a subatomic level has been observed for almost a century. It is my personal suspicion that practical enchantment is the scientific evidence the effect of our consciousness scales up from the subatomic to the physical world. What are magical results but a manipulation of real-world probabilities, after all?

The most important contribution quantum physics offers the world of magic is that it overturned centuries of discretism. It ended forever a materialist clockwork universe. And as Dean Radin, senior scientist at the Institute of Noetic Sciences, points out, it achieved this with surprising rapidity and ease ... in only three or four experiments. The whole industrial edifice of the Imperial Age was knocked over with a feather. So much for those prison bars, eh?

God Plays Dice with the Universe but She Uses D20s

We move now from the chaos of your subatomic parts to the impact of probability on your everyday life. French physicist Olivier Costa de Beauregard wrote, "It must be in the nature of probability to serve as the operational link between objective and subjective, between matter and psychism."[32] The question of why the physical universe expresses itself probabilistically is a deeper one than most. Developing a coherent answer to it qualifies you to found your own religion—and you will recall that I promised not to sell you a worldview. However, in between metaphoric bong rips, it is my suspicion that the universe's inherent *optionality* allows it to experience itself in the most effective way. "Divided for the chance of union," and all that.

Perhaps the main reason why Western magic handles probability so poorly is that most of its constituent parts predate probability, sometimes by millennia. Given that the Greeks gave us so much mathematics and

---

32   Olivier Costa de Beauregard. *The Second Principle of the Science of Time, Entropy, Information, and Irreversibility.* Seuil.,1963.

geometry, it is surprising they did not develop a theory of probability. A possible explanation as to why is twofold: their philosophical over-reliance on absolute truth proven via logic and axioms, as well as a more general sense that the future unfolded according to the will of the gods. Thus, to use mathematician Leonard Mlodinow's example, if an astragalus toss meant that a particular Greek boy would have to marry the stocky, plain Spartan girl he would not view the toss as lucky or unlucky but as the will of the gods.[33] (Today's more sophisticated magicians split the difference and see the will of the gods expressed probabilistically. Spousal selection techniques have also improved, albeit only marginally.)

We have thus inherited spiritual systems that fail to accurately measure risk or probability because they rely on spiritual beings as explanations rather than actors. That accounts for maybe a large minority of our complete mispricing of risk and reward. The majority of it appears to be a wholescale adoption of the "special snowflake" myth from the monoculture. This notion that you are in some sense entitled to a destiny or that you automatically "deserve" to have your dreams fulfilled is not well-supported in magic or Paganism's classical texts. We have diluted what is probably our most powerful asset, magical thinking, by confusing it with the advertising slogans you heard during the television programmes of your childhood. Nowhere is it written that you are guaranteed miracles on demand.

When it comes to selecting or determining preferred outcomes, there are two essential concepts that are frequently confused: possibilities and probabilities. It is *possible* that a billionaire with a heart of gold will leap from his limousine, dart through five lanes of traffic and propose marriage to you on your walk to work. But how probable is it? Failure to distinguish between these concepts is at the root of why the lottery may be legitimately called a tax on poor people.

---

33   Leonard Mlodinow. *The Drunkard's Walk: How Randomness Rules Our Lives.* Penguin, 2009.

It is almost instinctive to believe the most desirable *possibility* is also the most probable. The starlet-to-be who gets off the bus in Hollywood cannot but help believe that international fame is mere weeks away. But has she mispriced the risk in her preferred outcome? There is quite a string of low-probability events that need to happen in precisely the right order or overlap to deposit her on the red carpet out the front of Mann's Chinese Theatre. We will return to how a magician may best take advantage of this mathematic truth, but for now pay attention. *The probability that two events will both occur can never be greater than the probability that each event will occur individually.*

This is one of the three laws of probability and whilst it sounds counterintuitive, the math is really quite simple. Say you are trying to calculate how many respondents to a survey happen to be fathers. Your equation would look like this, with P as probability:

P(both male and parent) =
P(male) + P(parent) − P(either male or parent)

You see how if you do not subtract the "either" component then you are double-counting the respondents who fall into *both* categories. Mathematically this means the probability that our budding starlet is both a famous actress and lives in Los Angeles is less likely than either one occurring individually. How she achieves both outcomes in her life is best served by an awareness of this probabilistic reality. Secure, stable, low-cost housing in LA: one event. Secure career optionality in terms of salary, flexibility, and growth potential: a second event. Enchant continuously for an expanded network of theatrical and production people in a social capacity, at the very least. Then start thinking about auditions. Getting off the bus with a "make me famous" good luck charm tucked into her pocket is not the recommended approach.

Very much related to this challenge is what Nassim Taleb calls "the te-leological fallacy."[34] This is the dangerous illusion that you know exactly where you are going, and that you knew exactly where you were going in the past, and that others have similarly succeeded in the past by knowing where they are going. Across the magical world the teleological fallacy persists under the guise of one's "True Will." Apparently it is the magician's main challenge to merely *find* what his or her True Will or destiny or whatever happens to be.

The associated error in the teleological fallacy is the mistaken beliefs that *others* know what they want, where they are going, or—worst of all—what it is they will want tomorrow. Talking destiny or fatalistic outcomes with magicians is the very definition of the blind leading the blind. (But knowing this in advance makes going to parties thrown by occultists really quite fun.)

Hopefully by now you will have perceived that a more effective map is emerging, one that relies on an understanding of the probability of individual events versus their combinations and the inhibiting belief that you know, right from the outset, where you are going and how to get there. Moving in smaller, less defined steps offers you something that carries a tremendous amount of in-built mathematical energy: optionality. An option is not whether you choose the cake or the ice cream. Viewed from the perspective of pure theory, optionality allows you to benefit from the positive side of any uncertain situation without exposing you to any damage from the negative outcome of the same uncertainty.

The key benefit of wealth people always cite is that it confers freedom, when what they probably mean from a more precise perspective is optionality. A failure to understand this notion can lead to an over-accumulation of mortgage debt that traps you in unsatisfying employment to service

---

34   Nassim Nicholas Taleb. *Antifragile: Things That Gain from Disorder*. Penguin, 2013.

an oversized debt burden in a part of the world you do not wish to live because you believed—thanks to the teleological fallacy—that's how one builds wealth... which confers freedom. However, you have ended up with the complete opposite. Any stored optionality has been systematically destroyed.

The Emerald Hologram of Hermes Trismegistus

Goethe once wrote "he who cannot draw on three thousand years of history is living hand to mouth." This is a much more sophisticated way of thinking about which aspects of historic spiritual practices can enrich our modern lives than using terms such as "ancient wisdom." Because it is quite clear that any number of excellent ideas or concepts have tumbled down to us from the past. As we close out the chapter, our adventurer's map comes into view, and it looks like a universe in which consciousness is fundamental. Out of that first fundament, fizzing into existence first at the subatomic level, is a probabilistically expressed physical universe over which it appears we have some little control, as evidenced by the wealth of tantalising psi experimental results. In a June 2014 podcast interview with Disclose Truth TV, Dr. Russell Targ:

> *After forty years of research, the reality of ESP is so strong it would be statistically unreasonable to deny it. The evidence for ESP is ten times greater than the evidence that aspirin prevents heart attacks.* [35]

The demonstrable impact of consciousness across distances both temporal and spatial has a profound impact on how we describe reality. For psi effects to be achieved—and they are regularly achieved—there must be some operational connection between you and the rest of the universe. And I do mean *must*. There is no question mark after the statement "psi effects

---

35   Disclosure Truth TV, "Russell Targ Proof of Phychic [sic] Abilities," published to YouTube June 6, 2014. www.youtube.com/watch?v=X9cEpxXg3pA.

are real." And so any model of physics excluding the existence of consciousness/psi effects is both incomplete and inaccurate. Consider Nagarjuna's description of reality as Indra's net; an infinite web of diamonds where each individual stone contains and reflects an image of every other stone. It looks for all the world like a 200 CE version of the increasingly popular holographic universe theory. As most esotericists now know, every tiny piece of a hologram contains a complete version of the whole image. Here, then, is a possible interpretation of how psi effects may work across both time and space: whatever event you are seeking to influence or view is, in some metaphoric/holographic way, contained within you in its entirety.

For those familiar with it, this description bears a striking resemblance to the vision of creation described in the Hermetica: each microcosmic consciousness contains in miniature a version of the macrocosmic mind of God. One can inevitably get caught in an infinite loop looking for science to "prove" a mystical worldview, or have a mystical worldview "validate" scientific findings. In all cases these paradigms are, to paraphrase the Buddhists, fingers pointing at the moon, rather than the moon itself. What is important from the perspective of practical enchantment is that consciousness and the physical world appear to have areas of overlapping results.

Consider Dean Radin's famous experiments on mind/matter interaction at Burning Man festivals. Random number generators positioned around the festival recorded enormous deviations from the mean during peak events such as the burning of the man or the temple. The odds of this happening by chance are 106,420 to 1. In his book, *The Noetic Universe*, ponders the implications of psi experiment results.

> *After a century of slowly accumulating scientific evidence, we now know that some aspects of psychic phenomena are real. The importance of this discovery lies somewhere between an interesting oddity and an earth-shattering revolution. At a minimum, genuine psi suggests that what science presently knows about the nature*

of the universe is seriously incomplete, that the capabilities and
limitations of human potential have been vastly underestimated,
that beliefs about the strict separation of objective and subjective
are almost certainly incorrect, and that some "miracles" previously
attributed to religious or supernatural sources may instead be
caused by extraordinary capabilities of human consciousness.[36]

When it comes to navigating a consciousness-based probabilistic universe for fun and profit, a number of recommendations present themselves. Firstly, lean into optionality rather than charging off after lofty goals from a standing start. Take single steps rather than multiple steps to maximise your starting probability. At each step on the way to your goal, maximising optionality also maximises the probability of a preferred outcome for the next step. Make peace with the cognitive reality that you both probably do not really know what you want and *definitely* do not know the correct way to achieve it from the outset, so re-examine your options at each step and be open to the hitherto-unanticipated route.

Human consciousness clearly has an impact on the physical realm, but it is more reliable in nudging small, high-probability events than bringing down the walls of Jericho by the power of will. In a 1901 letter to fellow Golden Dawn magician Florence Farr, the poet W. B. Yeats wrote "whatever we build in the imagination will accomplish itself in the circumstances of our lives."

Which becomes especially true when you build one brick at a time. And while the bricks get smaller and smaller as you build, the next one— the cornerstone, if you will—is an absolute doozy.

---

36   Dean Radin. *The Noetic Universe*. Corgi, 2009.

BECOMING
INVINCIBLE

The purpose of life is to familiarize oneself with this after-death body
so that the act of dying will not create confusion in the psyche.

TERENCE MCKENNA

Properly used, magic will destroy your life. This is a feature, not a bug. Ever since modern humans first emerged into full consciousness those who worked with spirit, be they shamans or witches or magicians, moved into their tribal function only after some kind of Otherworld trauma experience. Some event has to occur that provides the magician with a lasting, visceral, unshakable *knowing* that the universe extends beyond what can be physically observed.

Pragmatically, I do not much care what that event is. The very fact that you are reading this book suggests you may have already had one: a UFO encounter, a poltergeist attack, a near death experience (NDE), a profound visit from a deceased relative. Really any event beyond common consciousness effects such as sibling telepathy will do. As you can see from the above list, they do not even need to be pleasant. If you feel the need to spend the night in an abandoned mental hospital with nothing but a Ouija board for company, go right ahead. For most of human history, shamanic initiations were—and still are—hugely traumatic. If you have been abducted by aliens or Discovery Channel has made a programme about ghosts in your house, then you can probably skip this chapter. Otherwise, read on.

"True" Initiation: Becoming Invincible

You are certainly free to join whatever nineteenth-century swingers club masquerading as a magical order you like, but do it on your own time. The purpose of this chapter is to provide options for "true" initiation, or what we otherwise might call *becoming invincible*. Why?

There is no greater defence against the grim, uncompromising wasteland of the late capitalist world than the unshakeable awareness that it will end and you will not. One of the most popular posts on my blog, *Rune Soup*, is called "There is the Rescue Mission and the Salvage Mission." Just as our Palaeolithic ancestors had to head out onto the ice or into the sea in tiny boats regardless of the weather, there is something simply and profoundly stabilising in knowing that you are so much more than your circumstances or your job that makes getting up at 5 am to go do some telemarketing a little bit more bearable. Becoming invincible is the process of immunising yourself against the monoculture. Your world becomes permanently bigger…so big that the shrill howlings of marketers and politicians get so faint that you can barely hear them, let alone believe them.

From a mythological perspective, becoming invincible begins with the inciting incident. Viewed in this context, an initiation ritual does not actually initiate you but rather triggers the process of initiation. It is the act of dialling the universe, not the moment when the universe actually picks up. You cannot simply draw a bath, light a few scented candles, and declare yourself a witch. Take your bath, but you are only a witch after the demons have come calling, which they most certainly will.

The Fastest Route

It's best to not sugarcoat this: the most effective route to becoming invincible is to take a high dose of psychedelics in a suitable ritual environment. And I do not mean most effective for you, because I don't even know you. I mean most effective overall. This was mankind's initiatory method of choice for at least thirty thousand years. Added together, all nonpsychedelic methods of shamanic initiation represent a small fraction of the whole. The so-called Palaeolithic Renaissance may represent the largest, longest psychological experiment mankind has ever performed, lasting ten millennia.

The last twenty or so years of archaeology are finally beginning to overturn the Victorian prudishness that has prevented us seeing these substances make the jump from hunter-gatherers to settled societies. Indeed, it appears humans first grew einkorn wheat to turn into beer rather than bread, and viticulture appears to predate agriculture. It is our thoroughly modern view of the past that obscures this reality. We think of marijuana or opium as "drugs" and leeks or carrots as "vegetables," but the classical world saw them all as plants. Some you ate, some stopped stomach cramps, some relieved pain. Their view of the plant kingdom was much broader with a greater range of outcomes that could be achieved in their dealings with it. We have missed this entirely. Consider the opinion of Dr. D. C. A. Hillman in *The Chemical Muse*.

> *Imagine how our views of the past would change if we knew that Plato enjoyed using psychedelics as a devotee of certain mystery religions, or that Alexander drank opium at his rowdy banquets, or that Julius Caesar smoked weed while preparing to cross the Rubicon...*

[F]ew academicians would even consider the possibility that the collected thoughts of the Classical world had been heavily influenced by the use of psychotropics. Despite innumerable references in the literature to plants containing mind-altering chemicals, despite precise descriptions in the same works of the effects of psychotropic substances on humans, and despite the documented use of narcotics in Classical medicine, modern scholars of all strains are culturally united by their unwillingness to admit that drugs had a significant impact on the evolution of Western literature.[37]

It was only in the decades immediately following World War II that it became legally problematic to do so, as the molecules became the subject of large-scale human testing by intelligence networks, their assets (including counterculture heroes Timothy Leary and Andrijah Puharich) and also became a cornerstone source of black project funding.

Magical publishing in the last thirty years has been significantly hamstrung by the way psychedelics have been used as geopolitical footballs. As an author, I cannot legally advocate a reader break any laws, and publishers can, in theory, be held liable for damages arising from actions taken as described in their books. This state of affairs has detached a generation of magical seekers from their palaeolithic birthright.

Fortunately, the drug laws of the western world are slowly returning to sanity over the protests of a pharma industry that would much rather sell you five years of antidepressants than have you cure yourself with a mushroom. So I can legally suggest you investigate an ayahuasca retreat in the Amazon conducted by a responsible local shaman. And I can legally suggest you consider a Santo Daime church experience or a psychedelic drumming circle outside Amsterdam. You can even visit one of the growing number of

---

37   D. C. A. Hillman, PhD. *The Chemical Muse: Drug Use and the Roots of Western Civilization.* Thomas Dunne Books, 2014.

states that have legalised marijuana and spend a supervised evening camping out in the woods, intoning a mantra of your choice.

Too often I hear that such a solution is unaffordable. This is an opportunity cost error. What is more important than becoming invincible? You may otherwise take five years of dedicated magical practice to achieve an effect of comparable profundity. Think of what the initiated you could have achieved with those five years. When people say "unaffordable," they mean "I don't want to change a single thing about my life, but please can I be a wizard?" Sell your television, move in with friends or family, sell your car. To paraphrase Doc Brown, where you're going, you won't need roads.

The Second-Fastest Route

You may consider a self-initiation ritual to be a safer choice than a ritualised psychedelic experience. You would be wrong. Fallout from becoming invincible is impossible to predict. Even if you are in the snake- and piranha-infested Amazon, at least you are in the safe hands of an experienced shaman!

Boiled down to its essence, a self-initiation is a declaration to the universe that you have a seat at the table, that your Highest is united with your Lowest, and you expect the cosmic croupier to deal you in. It is a fundamentally radical act, a transgressive move. It runs counter to almost two thousand years of social, economic, and religious diktat. There is a lot to burn through, which is why you must persist in your transgression until the volume of High Strangeness in your life is so extreme that it cannot be interpreted as anything other than *contact*.

One of the most notorious, simple and widely used methods of triggering initiation is found in Paul Huson's classic *Mastering Witchcraft*. In it, he suggests the aspirant light a candle just before bed for three successive nights and recite the Lord's Prayer backwards. The speaker is required to visualise shackles being struck off his or her arms as the incantation is read. Such a seemingly simple approach belies its potent psychological effect. Even those raised decidedly godless will still balk at such an inversion of cultural norms. It is a depatterning exercise *par excellence*.

Beyond depatterning, the violation of taboo or the transgression of cultural norms is an ancient and essential component of practical magic. In Laura Makarius's seminal article "The Magic of Transgression" (1974), she points out that tribal taboos reflect cosmic limitations imposed by the spirit world. For instance, it may be forbidden to eat the flesh of a certain animal because it is involved with a creation story. To temporarily break a taboo is to unleash tremendous power because the sorcerer steps outside the rules or conditions governing the proper function of reality. Returning to Philip K. Dick's metaphor of the black iron prison, transgressive magic temporarily bends these bars so that the witch may come and go as she pleases. Makarius explains further:

> *In magic based on the violation of taboo, the individual sees*
> *himself placed in a new relationship with regard to nature: instead*
> *of suggesting to natural forces what he expects of them, by relying*
> *on imitative acts, he wrests from them the power to coerce them*
> *into yielding to his wishes.*[38]

As we have seen, the economics of our reality are constructed in a way that favours a tiny elite at our expense. That leaves us with two metaphysical choices. First, use sympathetic magic to imitate the tiny elite in the hopes that such an imitation will eventually stick, but this is a gamble of very long odds. Second, use transgressive magic to break the system of economic harvesting. You know which one I am going to suggest.

In the spirit of Paul Huson's simple, transgressive trigger, below you will find a suggestion that more closely aligns with the economic challenges we currently face. The underlying function is identical.

---

38   Laura Makarius, "The Magic of Transgression." *Anthropos* Issue 69. 1974.

The Headless Rite

The association between headlessness and the spirit world stretches back up to fifty thousand years. Burials have been discovered with the skulls of the dead smeared in red ochre or detached entirely. Decapitation is the most important component of the shaman's metaphoric dismemberment. Symbolically this likely represents a shaman or witch having her head in another realm. It survives today in folklore across much of the planet. One need only think of John the Baptist, he who initiated Jesus Christ and brought God down to earth...a quintessentially shamanic act. His head was removed by the goddess (the Queen of Sheba) and has become one of the cornerstone treasures of western esotericism.

One of the more obvious continuities of African neolithic shamanism into dynastic Egypt is the story of Osiris. His is an archetypal shamanic role: dismembered and decapitated, hid in a tree to further emphasise his vegetative association, and then restored back to life through the magic of his sister/queen, to become the lord of the underworld—the home of the spirits—who also appears in the sky as the constellation Orion.

There is thus significant precedent for folding this imagery into an initiatory process. Fortunately for us all there is a ready-made, solo-rite version of this imagery hiding in plain sight of the western esoteric tradition. What is now known as *The Preliminary Invocation or Bornless Rite* was first translated from a collection of Greek Magical Papyri housed at the British Museum in 1852 and was subsequently discovered by magicians involved in the High Victorian renaissance—namely Samuel Mathers and Aleister Crowley. Despite some clumsy retranslation where the word "headless" was swapped out for the word "bornless" thanks largely to their penchant for playing fast and loose with Hebrew words when it suited them; the Hebrew *resh* can mean, among other things, "head" or "beginning," but the original Greek, *akephalos*, is clearly "headless."

Even with its transliteral damage, *The Stele of Jeu*—its other commonly known name—has still managed to accidentally trigger some of the most significant events in the last 125 years of Western magic. Crowley, for instance, performed it inside the Great Pyramid (which is probably a stone map of the Orion constellation on earth) during his honeymoon. He then performed it again when passing back through Egypt; both acts preceded the reception of the Book of the Law.

Dating in its current form to around the third century, the rite contains vivid elements of the Egyptian tradition—through the use of terms such as Osiris, Pharaoh (*paphro* in Greek) and general references to judgement and hating when unjust things happen—as well as the Hebraic tradition through the use of concepts such as Moses and Israel. We shall come onto this in later chapters, but it is during these centuries of extreme Hellenic hybridity that western magic begins to take on its recognised form. As a self-initiation rite, then, it ticks all the boxes.

Given that more august sorcerers than myself have messed around with it to great effect, I have provided a modification that includes the four kings of the grimoires. My reasoning behind this is, I think, sound. Directionality—specifically the honouring of directions—is another obvious continuation from Neolithic shamanism. Rather than simply opting for the more milquetoast option of "the four elements," the four kings are a better match for the rite's original spiritual goal. In conversation with the author Jake Stratton-Kent, the world's foremost authority on Goetia, he suggested that the rite is designed to associate its performer with a very large and powerful spirit that has the requisite authority over lesser spirits. It orients the magician in a higher position relative to an ambivalent spirit world. There is much to recommend this interpretation, especially when one reads of Osiris as king of the spirits of the Land of the Dead in the Pyramid texts. Also, Moses is the typological "law giver." His word—and thus the magician's word—is the word of God.

If any of this sounds too much like bullying spirits, I recommend taking the ayahuasca/shamanism route mentioned at the top of this chapter instead. It may serve to re-frame your opinion away from cartoon fairies at the bottom of an Edwardian garden more toward the intense and occasionally unpleasant realities of extradimensional contact. The spirit world is certainly holy, but that does not mean it is *nice*. Shamanism, for instance, is better described as "wrangling and trading" with the spirit world than anything we might consider worship. Besides, these bombastic phrases are more for the magician's benefit than the spirit's. We announce ourselves loudly and then we make friends.

The secondary reason for suggesting this rite as a means to triggering initiation is that it is largely interoperable with whatever your resting belief system happens to be. All too often when reading a magic book, the author seems hell-bent on converting you to his or her belief system. I have no such inclination. The Headless Rite deals with spirits and the spirit world. These concepts are for all intents and purposes universal. You do not need to swap out any of your gods or festivals to work it. You could take yourself off to mass or a sabbat or Diwali immediately afterwards.

Perform once and then see what happens over the ensuing couple of days. Then perform several more times, randomly and/or as needed. The rite may trigger initiation, but it is not an initiation rite. Like an old friend, you can return to it whenever you feel like it.

Preparation: Headless Rite

1. The only real requirements is a piece of paper or parchment on which to write the words of power:

   AŌTH ABRAŌTH BASYM ISAK SABAŌTH IAŌ

2. Be clean. Be in a space that is clean. (Optional if you are doing this someplace atmospheric like an abandoned train tunnel. Whatever floats your boat.)

3. As for candles and incense, these are largely theatrical. Use new candles if you are going to have any and probably stick to frankincense. For the Four Kings component, if you are performing this outside, I recommend some rum to pour out as an offering. If this is unachievable, then carry the incense with you to each quarter.

4. Locate the constellation Orion. I use one of the many available stargazing apps for this. Even during the daytime, just wave your phone around pointing at the ground until you find it. If anything, having the stars under the earth is more appropriate anyway. You will perform the rite in the direction of Orion.

The Headless Rite

Face north, touch your left temple and then your right temple with the parchment, and read aloud what is written on it six times:

AŌTH ABRAŌTH BASYM ISAK SABAŌTH IAŌ
AŌTH ABRAŌTH BASYM ISAK SABAŌTH IAŌ
AŌTH ABRAŌTH BASYM ISAK SABAŌTH IAŌ
AŌTH ABRAŌTH BASYM ISAK SABAŌTH IAŌ
AŌTH ABRAŌTH BASYM ISAK SABAŌTH IAŌ
AŌTH ABRAŌTH BASYM ISAK SABAŌTH IAŌ

Then say:

Subject to me all daimons, so that every daimon, whether heavenly or aerial or earthly or subterranean or terrestrial or aquatic, might be obedient to me and every enchantment and scourge which is from God.

(Note: If you invest in a nice piece of parchment and put some effort into the writing, the first part of the Headless Rite can be used in any number of situations, and the parchment itself becomes something of an apotropaic charm.)

Move from facing north to facing the direction of Orion and continue.

> *I summon you, Headless One, who created earth and heaven, who created night and day, you who created the Light and the Darkness; you are Osoronnophris whom none has ever seen; you are Iabas; you are Iapos; you have distinguished the just from the unjust; you have made female and male; you have revealed seed and fruits; you have made men love each other and hate each other.*
>
> *I am Moses your prophet to whom you have transmitted your mysteries celebrated by Israel; you have revealed the moist and the dry and all nourishment; hear me.*
>
> *I am the messenger of Pharoah Osoronnophris; this is your true name which has been transmitted to the prophets of Israel. Hear me, ARBATHIAŌ REIBET ATHELEBERSĒTH ARA BLATHA ALBEU EBENPHCHI CHITASGOĒ IBAŌTH IA; subject to me all daimons, so that every daimon, whether heavenly or aerial or earthly or subterranean or terrestrial or aquatic, might be obedient to me and every enchantment and scourge which is from God.*
>
> *I call upon you, awesome and invisible god with an empty spirit, AROGOGOROBRAŌ SOCHOU MODORIŌ PHALARCHAŌ OOO. Holy Headless One, deliver me from all restraining daimons and misfortune, ROUBRIAŌ MARI ŌDAM BAABNABAŌTH ASS ADŌNAI APHNIAŌ ITHŌLETH ABRASAX AĒŌŌY; mighty Headless One, deliver me from all restraining daimons and misfortune. MABARRAIŌ IOĒL KOTHA ATHORĒBALŌ ABRAŌTH, deliver me from all restraining*

daimons and misfortune, AŌTH ABRAŌTH BASYM ISAK
SABAŌTH IAŌ.

He is the Lord of the Gods; he is the Lord of the Inhabited
World; he is the one whom the winds fear; he is the one who made
all things by command of his voice.

Lord, King, Master, Helper, I call upon you, IEOU PYR IOU
IAŌT IAĒŌ IOOU ABRASAX SABRIAM OO YY EY OO YY
ADŌNAIE, immediately, immediately, good messenger of God
ANLALA LAI GAIA APA DIACHANNA CHORYN.

I am the Headless Daimon with sight in my feet; I am the
mighty one who possesses the immortal fire; I am the truth who
hates the fact that unjust deeds are done in the world; I am the one
who makes the lightning flash and the thunder roll; I am the one
whose sweat falls upon the earth as rain so that life can begin; I am
the one whose mouth burns completely; I am the one who begets
and destroys; I am the Favour of the Aion; my name is a Heart
Encircled by a Serpent; Come Forth and Follow.[39]

At this point, move to face east and continue on with the invocation
of the Four Kings. It is worth mentioning that you can effectively cut
the performance into two completely separate standalone rituals at this
juncture. I use a variant of the Four Kings ritual below as part of my
regular offering practice (more on that in later chapters). If you have
rum, pour out a quarter of it as you begin the invocation, otherwise
take the joss stick or censer with you as you perambulate the directions.

I invoke the Four Kings of the four corners of the earth. Most noble
and ancient spirits, be with me now.

---

39   Jake Stratton-Kent. "The Headless One." *Equinox*. Number 6. 1991.

*O Eastern Oriens, most shining, most excellent King, who
reigns over and commands the Eastern Regions, whose Kingdom
began with the founding of the world and shall endure until the
end of All Things. I conjure and invoke thee by the most high
and holy Names of God, do thou here manifest, clothed with all
thy power. Oriens, I conjure thee, by the virtue and power of the
Creator, and by the virtue of virtues.*

Turn around and face west. Pour out some rum. Continue.

*O Thou Paymon, King most glorious, who holds powerful
dominion in the Western Regions of the Heavens. I conjure and
invoke thee by the most high and holy Names of God, do thou here
manifest, clothed with all thy power. Paymons, I conjure thee, by
the virtue and power of the Creator, and by the virtue of virtues.*

Turn back to the north, pour some rum, and continue.

*O Thou Ariton, King most strong, whose Mighty Empire reaches
into the cold regions of the North. I conjure and invoke thee by the
most high and holy Names of God, do thou here manifest, clothed
with all thy power. Ariton, I conjure thee, by the virtue and power
of the Creator, and by the virtue of virtues.*

Face the south, pour the last of the rum, and continue.

*O Thou Amaymon, King most noble, ruler of the southern realms.
I conjure and invoke thee by the most high and holy Names of God,
do thou here manifest, clothed with all thy power. Amaymon, I
conjure thee, by the virtue and power of the Creator, and by the
virtue of virtues.*

Return to face the direction of Orion and finish.

> *I invoke you all with power and I pray to you with the authority of the One who spoke and who hath made all, and who, with one sole word gave birth to the world and whom all Creatures obey. By the Seat of his Majesty and by the great and august names of the Creator, most noble kings, I ask for your aid and blessing.*
>
> *By the holy name of IAŌ SABAŌTH, whose virtue hath no beginning and will have no end. So be it.*[40]

What Happens Next?

Good question. One thing I will say with every confidence is that your dreams will certainly get a lot more interesting. Beyond that it will really depend on the conditions of reality around you. Expect the most unbelievably remote coincidences to begin manifesting. Also expect that any attempt to explain how amazing these coincidences are will fall on deaf or unsympathetic ears. This is always the case with magic, as even when the preferred outcome manifests in the physical world, so much of its significance is inside your head.

In my own life, following on from regular, albeit sporadic practice of this exact rite, family-owned houses have sold for over a million dollars on the other side of the earth immediately after performing Four Kings offerings here in London. I have had—and turned down—job offers from out of the blue without even an interview, from the world's most desirable company. (Yes, that one.) The sensation is difficult to describe; it is almost as if you have dropped a depth charge into the ocean of the spirit world. Some things get cleared away, some things get shaken loose and some things come swimming.

---

40   Jake Stratton-Kent. *The Testament of St Cyprian the Mage.* Scarlet Imprint, 2014.

One of the most persistent fallacies of wealth magic (or "probability enhancement magic," as I prefer) is that the witch or sorcerer will work backwards from a successful result in her life and decide whatever combination of colour, scent, and godform does that thing. As such, I cannot promise you specific miracles as a result of this practice. All I can promise is that the stack of mostly positive, highly improbable events will one day get so heavy that all other explanations for how they happen collapse under the weight of their own mathematics. Then you can declare yourself invincible.

In fact, the question of how one becomes "truly" initiated in magic is perhaps the one I am asked more than any other. My answer is always the same.

Inevitably.

ARMIES OF
THE DEAD

I wish to debate the matter on the ground of experiments and observations
such as are appealed to in other inquiries for definite objective proof.

FREDERIC W. H. MYERS, FOUNDING MEMBER
OF THE SOCIETY FOR PSYCHICAL RESEARCH

This chapter has popped in and out of the book several times. My promise to you was to sell you as little of my personal belief system as possible. Working with the ancestors is probably the cornerstone of what you could consider my "resting belief system." There are two reasons why the chapter eventually made the cut. Firstly, ancestor veneration seems to be humankind's first spiritual practice and remains the most widespread so it is highly unlikely to upset anyone. The second reason probably will, however.

Consider that the primary form of enchantment associated with success magic is to do with having good luck through the wearing of luck charms or oils and so on. A chapter about dealing with the dead made it into the book because you will never find a more effective, broad-based, "luck" practice than providing offerings to your ancestors and the dead. The differences it will bring to your life are night and day.

I have no simplistic explanation for why this might be the case. There have been numerous studies on the psychological benefits of genealogy and becoming more aware of your own family story. Typically these are stress and anxiety reducing effects as your sense of self and identity becomes embedded in something bigger and more meaningful—an essential salve in today's isolated, modern world. These effects are certainly real, but they are only parts of a much greater sum. Properly enacted, chaos magic allows you to iterate through various magical forms until you land on ones that actually work, and incorporating ancestors and the dead into your sorcerous practices certainly fulfils that criteria.

Immortal Remains

It positively defines stuff white people like to suggest that other cultures have a somehow deeper understanding of ancestral spirits. This may be narrowly true today, but it is a much more recent phenomenon than most people realise. Most people involved in western magic are aware that at least some of the Catholic saints are direct adoptions of pre-Christian gods and goddess. Saint Brigid springs immediately to mind. However, viewed in their entirety, the saints are very obviously a continuation of the classical veneration of the honoured dead. When you consider that when they were alive, many local saints were effectively holy men and women—very useful in Dark Age communities—who are commemorated with the parading of their earthly remains or with specific foods and feasts, you can discern where this spiritual practice originates.

Adding to this are the regular masses said for deceased relatives, the existence of both family and community relics, and the persistence of folklore surrounding ghosts and spirits of place—it becomes apparent that we have been collectively ignoring our dead for only a very brief period of time. My personal suspicion as to why these practices never filtered into modern Paganism is that they were caught up in the identity politics of the postwar era where anything to do with the church was abandoned in favour of new gender and ecological perspectives. Whilst these perspectives were probably necessary, we threw the baby out with the bathwater and ended up paying for flights to Finland to have a shaman introduce us to our grandparents who were in front of our face the whole time.

Today's magicians must possess the sophistication to separate the paedophile banking component of the Vatican from the continuous cultural practices of our ancestors. What we might call "rural folk Catholicism" bears as much similarity to what happens before the throne of Saint Peter as the experience of flying on Air Force One has to you walking to your mailbox. At the folk level, you have the continuous survival of Mithras, Isis, the stars, the planets, and your own deceased relatives. Anyone looking to connect with an authentic, continuous magical practice really needs to get over their unexamined objection to church trappings and realise that this is the form that western European ancestral veneration (and eastern, for that matter) took for almost two thousand years. It is ahistorical to ignore it and "jump over the top" back into the classical world. Such an action is, by definition, a modern recreation.

One of the most potent ways of re-entering this ancestral tradition is through the largely ignored Catholic notion of the lonely soul, a stand-in for all the souls trapped in purgatory, trapped between this world and the next, an heuristic for all the spirits floating "out there," waiting for contact. Thanks to the work of writers such as Jake Stratton-Kent, we can see that there is a long-standing view of these spirits that has informed the entire western esoteric tradition. From the perspective of the magician, having the spirit work with him or her is part of her spiritual progress. We can read in numerous grimoires that the sorcerer promises to pray for the salvation of the wandering spirit they are seeking to summon. In *Discoverie of Witchcraft*, a ritual to summon what is effectively a fairy queen first requires summoning the spirit of a criminal on the promise of praying for its salvation and it is that spirit who fetches the sibyl for the magician.

"Salvation" in an early-modern context is closer to the exhortations of television psychics that souls must "move towards the light" than it is to any attempted post-mortem conversion to Christianity. There is a quid pro quo component to these interactions that is evidently very valuable to both sides and goes back thousands of years, perhaps even tens of thousands. In José Leitão's truly excellent *The Book of St Cyprian: The Sorcerer's Treasure*, the author points out that there is an implicit relation between the spirits the sorcerer frees from purgatory and the sorcerer him or herself. They become bound to him or her. Functionally, this is near-identical not only to the acquisition of magical assistants in the ancient world but also with the shamanic acquisition of spirit allies that must date back to before the Neolithic. Viewed from such a perspective, it becomes clear that the west has not really lost its spirit wisdom. We changed telephone providers but kept our old number.

The simplest way to begin with the spirits of the dead is to buy an Anima Sola/Lonely Soul statue or card, light a white candle before it and offer them spring water to quench their/his/her thirst. (Spring water makes the best offering for the spirits of the dead because it comes from under the ground.) Incidentally, this simple practice is also an effective way to "cool" minor poltergeist or spirit phenomena in a house or business.

A potentially more substantial way would be to visit a crossroad and begin a relationship with Saint Nicholas of Toletino, a thirteenth-century Italian mystic who spent years praying for and having visions of the souls in purgatory, ultimately becoming their patron. Much of his hagiography involves stories of ghosts and fetches. My favourite miracle attributed to him was the saving of nine souls caught in a sea storm. They prayed to him and he appeared floating in the sky, wearing his black Augustinian robes, with a lily in his left hand, radiating blinding, gold light. He waved his right hand and calmed the storm. Rock star.

Unlike so many saints who have made it into the western esoteric tradition, we know that Nicholas of Toletino physically existed. (Not that a lack of physical existence implies a lack of magical utility.) That may seem like a small point, but it is significant for the sections of the magical community that may have an aversion to Christian symbology. The practice of visiting the graves of dead mystics and wizards or otherwise asking for their aid predates Christianity by millennia. Whilst Nicholas's own beliefs were Christian, when viewed from a magical perspective we see a dead necromancer who continues to work for and with the dead. You could not ask for a better intercessionary being to begin or continue your relationship with them. His obscurity in the occult world needs to be rectified.

The Rite of Saint Nicholas

1. Take some spring water to a crossroads one evening (or buy a bottle on the way). Extra points if it is the evening of November 1, which is late on All Saints' Day and the night before All Souls Day.

2. Be sure you are alone, then tap the bottle three times on the ground.

3. Recite the following incantation. You are certainly free to de-church it if you like. But remember, even though we may not be Christian, Nicholas certainly was.

O merciful God,
In your providence you have chosen Saint Nicholas as a
special intercessor on behalf of the departed.

Take pity on those souls who have no particular friends
and intercessors to recommend them to Thee,
Who, either through the negligence of those
who are alive, or through length of time are
forgotten by their friends and by all.

Spare them, O Lord, and remember Thine own
mercy, when others forget to appeal to it.

Let not the souls which Thou hast created
be parted from thee, their Creator.

4. Pour the water out on the ground in the four directions and continue.

Most holy Saint Nicholas
May this offering bring refreshment
and hope to the souls in your care.

May the spirits of the dead remember
and look favourably upon me
As I remember and look favourably upon them.

May the souls of all the faithful departed,
through the mercy of God, rest in peace.

Amen.

Hidden in Plain Sight

It is difficult to conceive of just how disorienting the appearance of electric light, the beginnings of modern science and the eventual rise of Darwinism had on western worldviews. Before electric lighting, there was the sun or fire. For every single prior evening in all of human history, night was a time of dancing shadows. It seemed as if the world of magic was to be permanently obliterated by the march of science. Leading Victorian art critic John Ruskin put it thus in a letter to his friend at the time: "If only the geologists would let me alone, I could do very well, but those dreadful hammers! I hear the clink of them at the end of every cadence of the Bible verses."[41] But the dead are not so easily banished.

In 1882, the Society for Psychical Research was formed in London and continues to this day. At the time they advanced an idea whose radicalism has faded as the premise of materialism appears to be running its course. The idea was that you could develop a science of religion, that the spiritual experiences of the last thirty thousand years could be explored—if not quite *explained*—by recourse to these new scientific techniques.

Spiritualism is what happened when those early pioneers dragged a clunky electric light to the crossroads and illuminated the bones of our ancestors. It emerged in the years that overlapped the spirit customs of the pre-industrial age and the steam-powered ambition of the industrial one. It is a pivotal moment in the entire story of the western esoteric tradition that we have largely mistaken as being the *end* of it. The magical community's view of spiritualism has been shaped by the opinions of Victorian occultists such as Aleister Crowley—for whom it must be remembered spiritualism was *competition*—and the general sexism that it is little more than a hobby for grieving widows. It isn't. French Kardecism would go on to have a huge impact on the colonial spiritualities of the New World. Ouija boards outsold copies of Monopoly in 1967.

To dismiss Spiritualism is to dismiss the uninterrupted thread of western spirit relationships tracing back thirty thousand years. It is also to dismiss some supremely useful evidence that hearkens back to the previous chapter's goal of becoming invincible and may even have magical praxis implications.

---

41   Deborah Blum. "Those Dreadful Hammers." *Wired*. Accessed April 12, 2015.
     www.wired.com/2010/11/those-dreadful-hammers/.

The Scole Experiments

If ever the Society for Psychical Research had a case that deserved your undivided attention, it would be the Scole Experiments in the 1990s in the east of England. It is widely regarded as the society's most important case ever. (There are numerous, full-length documentaries on YouTube, and the book is readily available secondhand.) Observed phenomena included:

- Writing and symbols appearing on factory-sealed rolls of film left on the table.

- Apported objects, including newspapers from 1944 that were printed in processes not used since the seventies, on paper that was lacking chemicals it would otherwise have contained but didn't because of the war.

- Rose petals appearing on camera at séances at the Bacci Centre in Italy.

- Over the several years that the sessions occurred, they were attended by astrophysicists, NASA scientists, mathematicians, criminologists, and lawyers. (The astrophysicists went on to form their own study group.)

From a magical perspective, two components of the Scole Experiments have escaped wider notice and they seem significant to me. Firstly, the core group engaged in twice-weekly séances for more than a year with just minor phenomena before the extreme manifestations began. Secondly, the entities making contact with the group—who came to be known as "the spirit team"—required this initial sustained contact and chose to escalate the communication for their own reasons… which were to provide definitive evidence that human consciousness survives physical death.

Right here we can discern the magical need for regular contact with the spirit world. It enables us to boost the fidelity of the signal. Somewhere in the one hundred and thirty years of SPR experiments we begin to see the "evidence" that sustained contact with the spirit world "works better" than sporadic requests for assistance. This may well be the key to why incorporating the ancestors and the honoured dead has such a beneficial impact on the probabilistic outcomes of your life.

Near-Death Experiences

If it seems to you that near death experiences (NDEs) are a modern phenomenon then you are largely correct. We can find examples in historical literature that match the accounts that are now commonly reported, but they are scarce. There are also individual retellings such as the ones that temporarily capture the public's imagination in today's world. Individual experiences are certainly life-changing for those who go through them— and legitimately qualify as becoming invincible—but they remain anecdotal for the rest of us, interesting, not definitive. However, we are now closing in on five decades of accumulated data from which we may draw some fairly firm hypotheses.

Five decades? Prior to 1967, if you had a heart attack, you almost certainly died. But from 1967 onwards, portable defibrillators began to be used in emergency medicine. Since that time, the cause of death that is the most likely to trigger an NDE is cardiac arrest, because it is the cause of death that can most easily be reversed in a triage situation. It was only from 1975, when Dr. Raymond Moody published his bestselling *Life After Life*, that we even have the term "near death experience."

The most common way materialists dismiss NDE evidence is to claim that a brain starved of oxygen begins to hallucinate lights and colours, similar in experience to when jet fighter pilots black out during extreme manoeuvres. Even from a materialist perspective, such dismissals do not hold the slightest volume of water. Firstly, a single incident in which it can be demonstrated that a patient undergoing an out-of-body experience (OBE) or NDE returns with information they could not possibly have—such as in cases where the patients leave their bodies in operating theatres and travel to their family homes, returning with accounts of what transpired—obliterates the oxygen-starvation hypothesis. And there have been thousands of such incidents. Secondly, OBE/NDEs have occurred when patients have been inside MRI machines that can prove there was zero brain activity, so how could the brain be hallucinating? As for hallucinations—which certainly do happen during medical procedures—the defining characteristic of an NDE is that it is the most vivid and most real experience of the patient's life... which does not sound like a sputtering hallucination of a dying, anesthetised brain.

Dutch cardiologist Pim van Lommel—who studied NDEs in a clinical setting for more than twenty years and published his data in the esteemed medical journal *The Lancet*—explains the challenge to the "brain hypothesis" in his highly recommended *Consciousness Beyond Life*:

> *We still do not know how it is possible for people to experience an enhanced consciousness during a cardiac arrest, that is, during a period when the brain displays no measurable activity and all brain function, such as bodily and brain-stem reflexes and breathing, has ceased. Looking at the interaction between consciousness and the brain, we concluded that consciousness cannot be seen as the product of brain function. In fact, sometimes the opposite seems to apply: the mind influences brain function, both in the short and long term as a result of the empirically proven principle of neuroplasticity. Our current scientific knowledge cannot account for all aspects of the subjective experiences reported by some cardiac arrest patients with complete loss of all brain function.*[42]

Because of improvements in medical resuscitation, the number of NDEs is actually increasing. Dr. van Lommel estimates that 4 percent of the

---

42   Dr. Pim van Lommel. *Consciousness Beyond Life*. HarperOne, 2011.

total population has experienced one, which is about 9 million Americans and 20 million Europeans. From a magical perspective this is hugely fascinating as there has never been such a high number of Otherworld ambassadors in all of human history. Although the metaphysical community has largely ignored the available data, any of our wizardly predecessors would have positively leapt at the insights afforded by them. According to linguist and author Georgi Mishev, Bulgarian folk magic—a more or less continuous evolution of Thracian magical customs—treats what we call NDEs very seriously.[43] Of all the ways one can become a healer in the Bulgarian folk tradition, being close to death through illness or trauma and then returning is the most potent. In Bulgarian, they are called *preneseni*, which literally means "transferred." Those who are "transferred" back are believed to have powers of healing and prophecy, often taught to them by ancestors, saints, the Blessed Virgin, etc. Whilst the research that modern patients who have undergone NDEs have significant life improvements in terms of happiness, reduced anxiety, and so on is very robust, the contemporary Western world is not really in a position to quantify whether these experiences result in improved magical ability. It strikes me as a missed opportunity.

Although such a term would presumably cause mild discomfort to the hundreds of medical practitioners around the world diligently researching NDEs, we really must see the field as a continuation of the Western tradition of spiritualism. Near death experiences sit in that liminal zone between the estimable achievements of modern science and our shared spiritual heritage pertaining to the dead and their influence on our lives. From a chaos magic perspective, the data they offer afford us an unparalleled opportunity to calibrate our necromantic practice with some seemingly quantifiable evidence. On a personal level, the final nail in the coffin of "the brain as generator of consciousness" for me was learning that there are cases of

---

43   Georgi Mishev. *Thracian MagicPast and Present:* Avalonia, 2012.

blind people having NDEs who leave their bodies and are able to visually describe objects and faces in the operating theatre. Explain that one to me if these phenomena are simply a case of waking up during surgery!

Here are some of the other insights from Dr. Lommel's 2001 study published in the *Lancet*, which encompassed 344 patients in ten Dutch hospitals over a thirteen-year period.[44] Eighteen percent reported some recollection of the time during which they were unconscious. Of that 18 percent:

- 12 percent had significant NDEs and 21 percent had what was described as "superficial" NDEs (in the sense that they were light).
- The long-term life effects that arose among those that had NDEs were overwhelmingly positive, including a greater appreciation for love and family, reduced anxiety, and more.
- 50 percent had an awareness of being dead.
- 24 percent had OBEs.
- 31 percent reported moving through a tunnel.
- 13 percent experienced a life review.
- 31 percent described meeting with dead relatives.

Beyond the actual awareness of being dead—which is presumably a prerequisite for entering the Otherworld—the *greatest percentage* experience was meeting dead relatives … meeting ancestors. Imagine that.

Ancestral Altar

You probably already have an ancestral altar. Paintings or photographs of deceased relatives sitting upon a mantle are a direct continuation of a

---

44 Dr. Pim van Lommel. "Near-death experience in survivors of cardiac arrest: a prospective study in the Netherlands." *The Lancet*. Volume 358, No. 9298. December 2001.

20,000 year tradition of the removal of skulls of the dead to be set in the dwelling places of our palaeolithic ancestors. Viewed in such a way, it is only polite to maybe make them a little bit nicer: perhaps a cloth, some flowers, and some glassware only used to provide offerings to your ancestors. Available evidence suggests it is these beings who will meet you on the other side of the tunnel. Who else is more likely to have your back in this life?

Ancestor veneration does not rely on either the matching of blood types or moving sequentially back up your family tree. Adoption, for instance, was a common classical custom and—when it came to highborn families—was regularly undertaken specifically so that the adoptive parents would have someone to perform ancestor rites. You also do not need to know all or even any of the names of your ancestors to begin such a process. Modern adoptees are by no means excluded from ancestor work. In fact, they technically have around double the ancestors as nonadoptees. (Two family trees, you see.)

In situations of family trauma or childhood abuse it is important to realise that you are under no obligation to include *all* family members or ancestors on your altar. There is an unbroken chain of blood stretching from you right back to the first human on earth. Skip entire generations if you feel it appropriate. Having one's name or memory erased after death as a result of misdeeds in life was a very common and truly terrifying punishment in ages past. It remains very satisfying to mete out.

Hermanubis

Ah, Hermanubis, the most magically useful god you have never heard of. Emerging from the sometimes-literally psychedelic period of Greco-Egyptian syncretism, Hermanubis is a hybrid form of the Egyptian funerary god, Anubis, and the Greek messenger-trickster, Hermes. The combination of the two provides a psychopomp *par excellence*. He is depicted as having the body of Hermes and the head of Anubis. His most famous surviving statue is viewable in the Vatican Museum.

Cynocephalic (dog-headed) gods are supremely ancient and wide-spread. As for Hermanubis specifically, his origin is something of a moving feast. Plutarch, for instance, identifies Anubis with Hermes and with the star Sirius (the dog star). But the dog/messenger/Sirius connection is found at least as far back as the early New Kingdom where we see cyno-cephalic figures greeting the rising sun at the four doors of the eastern horizon on one of Ramses II's obelisk. The rising of Sirius marked the beginning of at least two of Egypt's simultaneous calendar systems. Firstly, the return of Sirius to the eastern skies in late summer after a seventy-day period (the same length of time as the mummification procedure) heralded the flooding of the Nile, the natural phenomenon responsible for Egypt's bounteous agricultural harvest. Secondly, Egyptian sacred calendars ran on a much longer year, the Sothic year—named for the heliacal rising of Sirius/Sothis—lasting 1,461 solar years.

This calendric notion survives into the Egyptian concept of the decans—mighty spirits that hold sway over sections of the night sky. The sequence of decans begins with Hermanubis, and here we can see his role as psychopomp and opener of the ways. He appears from the underworld and travels across the sky at the head of the entire parade of star gods.

From here, the whole notion of Sirius/dog/initiator and the late summer skies is absorbed into the mythology of the early European church. If you look at the calendar of saints from the end of July to the beginning of September, it is filled with dogs. Most famously is Saint Christopher, beloved of mad taxi drivers and mothers with large prams the world over, on July 25. His hagiography states explicitly that he was a giant from the land of Chananeans/canines whose only form of communication was barking. In southern France you find Saint Roch, August 17, and Saint Guinefort, who was/is an actual dog, on August 22. Another direct continuation of Hermanubis is found via Saint Bartholomew on August 24. In *Myths of the Dog Man* by David Gordon White (no relation), we read:

*[W]e find a version of the Coptic Acts of Bartholomew with a Latin
codicil… The codicil reads: "These are the acts of Bartholomew who,
upon leaving the land of Ichthyophages, went to Parthos with Andrew
and Christianus, the cynocephalic man." A similar codicil is found
much earlier, in the approximately fifth-century Syriac version of the
acts of Matthew and Mar Andrew: it says that the apostles converted
the "City of Dogs, which is 'Irqa,'" situated north of the Crimea.*[45]

Given that there is zero archaeological evidence for any of these people and a growing academic theory suggesting that much of the Christian
story is a retelling of star lore (twelve apostles, twelve zodiacal houses,
and so on), then "converting the City of Dogs" *could* represent the incor-
poration of the Sirian corner of the sky into the emerging religion. Saint
Christopher's feast day falls on the ancient ritual known as the *kunophon-
tis*, the "massacre of the dogs," a sacrifice performed to appease the restless dead ancestors of Apollo's son, Linos, who was killed and eaten by
dogs. It was quite common to see cynocephalic statues of Christopher at
the gates to European cities right up until the Middle Ages. Here we have
the "way opener" meet the dog-headed crosser of boundaries and spiritual insight. Before our very eyes, Hermanubis has continued along with
us in the march of western culture.

Christopher is the only cynocephalic being in the post-Christian western world to be given a name, although there have been dog "races" and
"people" for centuries. These peoples are from Libya, Egypt, northern
India, and the Horn of Africa, which most of the time was considered the
same place. Thus cynocephaly was a visual shorthand for eastern spiritual
influence. Interestingly, it currently appears that dogs were first domesti-
cated in southeast Asia.

45   David Gordon White. *Myths of the Dog Man.* University of Chicago Press, 1991.

Other direct continuities are found in Origen's accounts of the beliefs of the heretical gnostics. He writes that the gnostics believe "men ... [after death] assumed the shapes of these theriomorphic spirits and were called lions, bulls, dragons, eagles, bears and dogs."[46] Note that all these animals can be found in the constellations of the classical world, giving us a very poignant indicator of where the gnostics located their afterlife—among the stars. Returning to David Gordon White:

> The cynocephalic Hermanubis and Erathoath (Hermes-Thoth) are products of the Greco-Egyptian astrological tradition, and we may further glimpse, in the Coptic commemoration of Bartholomew's martyrdom on the first day of the month of Thot (August 29), an evocation of that animal-headed Egyptian deity whose symbolism was carried over into the Hellenistic world in the figure of Hermes Trismegistus. Second-century Alexandrian coins depict Hermes-Thoth together with cynocephalic apes and the caduceus, and another Ophite source, an "Abraxis" gemstone, depicts the cynocephalic Hermanubis holding a sceptre in each hand and standing between a half moon and a star, on the other side is the archon Michael. These Hellenistic traditions were the sources of Christian zoomorphic depictions of the four evangelists as well: these first spread from Asia Minor and the Coptic Christians of Egypt into Sicily, Visigoth Spain, Merovingian Southern France, and Celtic Ireland, with the cynocephalic Christopher hard on their tails.

Why dogs, death, and late summer? Why would this be my recommended route into magical dealings with the dead? This is a very, very old Indo-European association ... possibly a dozen millennia old. In numerous Indo-European traditions, the dead are compared to a herd or

---

46   White, *Myths*.

flock, with a divine shepherd and his dog or dogs managing the herd. We see echoes of this tradition with Hekate—to whom dogs are sacred—hounding lost souls; we see it with Cerberus guarding the threshold to the underworld; we see it in the Roman tradition of household gods and spirits, Lares, often depicted wearing dog-skins. In book XXII of *The Iliad*, Homer describes Sirius as the hound of Orion. During the dog days, Orion's hound "redoubled the fiery heat of the sun, bringing, in the afternoon, suffering to all living creatures."

Suffering and illness are consistently associated with the dog days and their presiding spirits. The origins of this connection are likely functional. Even today, high summer is a time of mosquitoes, viral outbreaks and water-borne illnesses, the baking heat leading us to drink from smaller and more dubious water sources. Thus the threshold between the former year and the new year was fraught with sickness and danger. It was and for much of the world still is a dangerous, liminal time. Liminality gave both Hermes and Anubis some of their many titles. In some places, Anubis held the title of *Apherou*, meaning "way-opener." Hermes had many similar titles such as *Psychopompos*, meaning "conductor of souls." You could not find a better hybrid to deepen your interactions with the dead. Following are several ways you can do that.

Working with Hermanubis

One of the purposes of running you through cynocephalic history at some length is to announce that you can get yourself a statue of Saint Christopher from almost anywhere and have a ready-made, almost-hoodooized home for Hermanubis on your altar. (Ideally, try to find one with a lamp, a sacred symbol of Hermes.) I traded up to a Saint Christopher from my previous print-out of the statue of Hermanubis from Wikimedia I put in a dollar store frame. Both work, but Chris looks better among my other god dollies.

Suggested offerings include spring water (obviously), rum, and aquavit. Suggested incense is storax or myrrh. Job done.

1. Open/banish as you see fit. The Headless Rite from the earlier chapter fits extremely well here on account of the connection between Osiris and Anubis.

2. Fire up the candles, incense, etc. Have a small shot glass in front of the statue and your liquid offering to hand. (The shot glass and liquid offering can be replaced with a bowl and wine as described below.)

3. Recite this modified spell from Betz's translation of the Greek Magical Papyri:

> *Hail Hermanubis! Come to me!*
>
> *O high one, O mighty one, O master*
> *of secrets for those in the Underworld,*
>
> *O Pharaoh of those in Amenti, O Chief Physician, O Good*
> *Son of Osiris, he whose face is strong among the gods.*
>
> *You should appear in the Underworld*
> *before the hand of Osiris.*
>
> *You should serve the souls of Abydos in order*
> *that they live through you, these souls,*
> *the ones sacred to the Underworld.*
>
> *Come to the earth! Reveal yourself to me here today.*
>
> *You are Anubis. You are Hermes. You are the one*
> *who went forth from the heart of the great*
> *Agathodaimon, the father of the father of all the gods.*

Come to the mouth of my vessel/indwell
in this form dedicated to you[47]

And receive my offering and praise. For I am Isis the Wise,
the sayings of whose mouth shall come to pass.[48]

Some notes on possibly unfamiliar terms: Amenti is the Western Lands (of the Dead). As for Agathodaimon, it was originally a Greek presiding spirit of vineyards and wine, but by this point in history had been syncretized with Serapis and the Logos, thus stitching together wine, dying, resurrecting gods, and the creation of the universe, which should sound very familiar. (Consider Jesus descending into hell to free all the Pagans who died before his appearance on earth, for instance.) Here is a highly fruitful line of enquiry I commend to you but sits outside the scope of this book.

The spell indicates the invocation should be repeated seven times. That is certainly recommended for your first few run-throughs. Eventually you will get the ship in the air faster than that, so to speak. From here, the rite splits. If it is a standard offering, then continue as below. If it is the bowl spell, jump to the next point.

Hermanubis, bring in a table for the gods. Let them sit.

Hermanubis, bring in a table for
the Honoured Dead. Let them sit.

Hermanubis, bring in the bread and wine for the gods,
bring in the bread and wine for the Honoured Dead.

Let them eat, let them drink.[49]

---

47 If making a standard offering, use first half of this phrase; if doing the "bowl spell," use the second half.

48 Hans Dieter Betz. *The Greek Magical Papyri in Translation Including the Demotic Spells. Second Edition.* University of Chicago Press, 1997.

49 Ibid.

Here is the part where Hermanubis becomes extremely useful and directional when it comes to speak with specific groups of the dead. For example, "Hermanubis, bring in a table for the spirits of the priests of Heliopolis" or "the spirits of the ancestors along my Portuguese bloodline."

You can also use this invocation at the beginning of a séance, for instance. Or you can call in a particular group of spirits simply to feed and honour them, and/or communicate with them via cartomancy.

Note: Offerings should be left on the altar/in the ritual space for a respectable length of time, such as overnight. Remove any foodstuff before it spoils. Ancestral offerings can be disposed of as you would any leftover foodstuff for your family (which is what they are). Err on the side of caution with offerings for other spirits and leave them at crossroads, in graveyards, or other between-spaces not located on your property. Much as on the African plains or in the open ocean, there is something of a food chain when it comes to spirit offerings. The big ones eat first. Then the others do. You do not want to be feeding or attracting the others to your house.

Another Offering Rite

Another adaptation from the Greek Magical Papyri. The spell calls for brass, but I picked up a copper curry bowl on Brick Lane in East London and use that instead. I'm nothing if not opportunistic/cheap/hungry.

1. Paint or use a silver permanent market to inscribe APHEROU (Way-Opener) on the inside base of the bowl.

2. If you wish to use it for direct scrying, light the candles, put the bowl on your lap, pour in spring water (or sea water to reach the souls of the dead lost at sea) followed by green olive oil, or only green olive oil with no water, and ask Hermanubis to show you what you seek. This works best in the low light environment that only magical candles can bring!

3. If you wish to ask Hermanubis for something specific like the blessing and support of the spirits of the Phoenician dead in your international business endeavour, then have wine rather than water or aquavit on hand. Pour it into the bowl and recite the following:

> *You are wine, you are not wine*
> *But the head of Anubis.*

> *You are wine, you are not wine,*
> *But the feet of The Messenger.*

> *You are wine, you are not wine,*
> *But the guts of Osiris,*
> *The guts of IAO SABAOTH*
> *APHEROU ABRASAX.*

Then speak your request to Hermanubis.

Once done, be sure to bid all assembled beings depart in peace and mutual respect. Disposal of the offerings is as above. Often I just let the spring water completely evaporate.

The Grateful Dead of Baar

I appreciate some fairly bold claims regarding the continuity of practices pertaining to the dead and ancestors have been made in this chapter, so let us close with the story of the Grateful Dead of Baar. The earliest version of this tale is from a thirteenth-century German book of miracles, the *Dialogus Miraculorum*.

Once there was a man from Baar who would always stop and offer up a prayer for the dead every time he walked past his local churchyard. It came to be that he was pursued by armed bandits one evening, so he ran into the churchyard to hide among the tombstones. The bandits followed him in, whereupon all the graves flung open, the dead rose and came to the defence of the man who prayed for them, wielding swords and great-staffs. The bandits fled in terror, never to bother the man from Baar again.

This story was popular right across Europe for several centuries. The scene was regularly depicted in churches as far away as Sweden. It served as a potent reminder to the faithful that the dead are never quite gone. In the twenty-first century we are fortunate enough to have more than one hundred years of empirical observations suggesting the same thing. The combination of knowing that *you* survive death, along with your ancestors and the heroic dead, is an immovable backstop that provides you with the courage to move forward in all fields of life.

And sure, you *could* probably pursue success without a skeleton army, but where is the fun in that?

AMBIVALENT ALLIES: TRIGGERING SYNC

> The believer's mistake is to ascribe meaning and credence to the secondary
> perception, the mental image created by our brain to account for the
> stimulus. The skeptic's mistake is to deny the reality of the stimulus
> altogether, simply because the secondary perception seems absurd.
>
> ————
>
> JACQUES VALLEE, *CHALLENGE TO SCIENCE*

In July of the year 1085, some shepherds on a mountain in the Spanish re-
gion of Navarra witnessed something very unusual in the night sky, something we might have categorised slightly differently today. The Blessed
Virgin and "a great star" descended upon them. The area quickly became a
site of pilgrimage. The king of Aragon and Navarre, Sancho Ramirez, paid
to have a shrine built on the spot. A sign on the chapel reads:

This is the Star
That came down from the Sky
To Estella
To observe it.

Creepy, right? Creepy and suggestive of the unavoidable reality that whatever the phenomena we call gods or angels actually *are*, they demonstrate tremendous fluidity in their chosen manifestations … fluidity to the point of deception. Philosophers including Patrick Harpur refer to these experiences as "daimonic phenomena," that is, phenomena that sit in the overlapping space between mythology, real physical manifestations, and psychic or paranormal experiences. Faeries, angels, and the Blessed Virgin Mary are probably the best western examples of the daimonic. Consider this observation from Dr. Roney-Dougal in *The Faery Faith*:

> *The Daimonic is linked to our world, but not of this world. This is illustrated by the curious link between a person's experience with [faeries] and the progress of human technology, the daimonic always being different in their technology from us. They are either more advanced than us in some way, as in their ability to appear and disappear, or less advanced, as in their medical technology. For example, the fair folk always seem to dress and have a culture from a time earlier than ours, and their "superiority" lies solely in their magical abilities.*[50]

For what I can only assume are personal reasons, a lot of occultists shy away from observing their gods in the much wider context of global paranormal, psi, and UFO phenomena. But we are required to look at the dataset as an overlay on both the probabilistic nature of the universe and indeed the changed probabilities of manifesting wealth and success in our current regime. We are looking for areas that can be *pushed* or *optimised*.

---

50 Serena Roney-Dougal. *The Fairy Faith*. Green Magic, 2003.

The most common answer you will hear to the question of which spirits or gods have the best affinity with wealth accumulation in the west are often the same beings associated with laws and royalty. Imagine that. We went to some length explaining how wealth gets harvested upward through the machinations of lawmakers, tax collectors, monarchs, and so on. Jupiter may well be the god of wealth, but he is not the god of you—he is a king's god, and his inherent conflict of interest did not go unnoticed amongst the Romans, either. As they moved from a monarchy to a republic, the consuls would still swear an oath to Jupiter; the ancient god of kingship and high-born families. It is an ancient version of "the more things change, the more they stay the same" and it presents some operational challenges. Modern magic has also mistaken the much, much later astrological Platonic system—a long-defunct explanatory model of the universe—for an eternal conception of Jupiter (or Hermes, et cetera). This is akin to thinking the gun totin' cowboy Jesus of twentieth-century America is the same Jesus the Christian apologists were trying to embed into European philosophy.

Do these political complications mean we should avoid such beings? Perish the thought. What is required, however, is a little discernment.

If you choose to go full conspiracy on your geopolitics, the world is controlled by a tiny, kingly elite that is not running the place for your benefit. If you choose not to go full conspiracy, the world is a chaotic morass of unbalanced and competing agendas fighting over dwindling resources and vanishing jobs. However you slice it, an orderly, lawful, presiding deity of wealth accumulation is not the best ally and may even be asleep at the wheel. You need an ally who is wilier, who is ambivalent. You need someone who can trick. From *The Trickster and the Paranormal*:

> *Trickster figures have particular appeal to marginal (low status)*
> *groups. In ancient Greece, aristocrats viewed merchants and*
> *craftsmen with suspicion and disdain. Norman Brown notes in his*
> Hermes the Thief *(1947) that "Hermes symbolized the aspirations*

of the non-aristocratic classes"; in fact Hermes was the patron of merchants. A similar situation was seen in the Middle Ages. As feudalism began to crumble, some of the nobility no longer enjoyed the privileges they once did. The merchants' plight improved, but their social position was unsettled, because their status was not bound to the class of their birth. The feudal and church authorities distrusted them, and fittingly, Reynard the Fox, a trickster, was their symbol. All this illustrates the nexus of merchants, liminality, unsettled status, and the trickster.[51]

In a probabilistic universe, an ambivalent ally accompanying you on the climb is much more useful than a lawful, cosmic throne before which you are expected to beg. Shoot for *luck*, not power; shoot for *tricks*, not clout. Too often we pray for the proverbial miracle, the very low probability outcome, when instead we should be nudging and swapping for smaller goals with nearby spirits.

The advent of affordable computing over the last forty years has uncovered some fascinating insights into how we really go about achieving objectives. The most important of these insights has to do with the limitation of top-down control. From *Obliquity* by economist John Kay:

In general, oblique approaches recognise that complex objectives tend to be imprecisely defined and contain many components that are not necessarily or obviously compatible with each other, and that we learn about the nature of the objectives and the means of achieving them during a process of experiment and discovery. Oblique approaches often step backwards to move forwards.[52]

---

51   George P. Hansen. *The Trickster and the Paranormal.* Xlibris, 2001.

52   John Kay. *Obliquity: Why Our Goals are Best Achieved Indirectly.* Profile Books, 2011.

In your own lives you will know that the big goals never go even slightly according to plan. Just think back to what you thought your career would look like before it even began. Oblique approaches not only accommodate such inevitable chaos into your journey, they often draw strength from them. We require nimble feet. Winged, even. Where have we heard that before? Oh yes, the classical pantheon (and to a lesser extent the logo of a large flower-delivery company). The name Hermes derives from the ancient Greek term for the small piles of stones used to mark out the borders between properties. He stands on the boundary and can move freely between them, between the worlds, so to speak. This is a common characteristic of the Trickster; his or her unpredictable location as well as what he or she *brings back* from that other Place. Hermes has his own power of prophecy, but unlike some of the more upstanding denizens of Olympus, his manifests through games of chance rather than profound statements from on high. This is the quintessence of High Strangeness, of the paranormal, of mostly beneficial coincidences.

Tricksters are often possessed of the knowledge of the whole earth as well as the means to subvert the rules that keep the magician away from what he or she wants. Stories of Brer Rabbit in the folklore of the southern United States and his regular triumphs over much more powerful animals come to mind. Wakdjunkaga, the Winnebago trickster, refers to every object and animal on earth as "younger brother." He predates them and is thus possessed of the full knowledge of everything in creation. A similar belief is attached to the devil in Iberian magic. According to José Leitão, the devil's capacity to intervene in people's lives comes not from some inherent evil power, but from his great age.

Tricksters rule the liminal space, the territory of the shaman. Between the manifest and the unmanifest, night and day, male and female. Just as the shaman does, the trickster crosses boundaries for us and *if it so chooses*, returns with something we need or want. Tricksters represent a high degree of uncertainty, unpredictability, and obliquity. A skilled magician can ride a trickster to his or her life goals without having to spell out the hundreds of dreary steps in between (which will be wrong anyway). Pete Carroll puts this obliquity quite succinctly in *The Octavo*.

> *Conjure then, for needs if must, but preferably for opportunity and quality of experience, but never merely for more of the same.*
>
> *Conjure not for wealth, but for the experiences that you would spend the wealth on if you had it. Any necessary wealth will then materialise as a side effect.*[53]

Practical enchantment manifests most often as beneficial synchronicities rather than bombastic, miraculous appearances of gold bars falling from the sky. So your objective should always be to increase the total volume of positive synchronicities in your life. These are both simultaneously the signals of and opportunities offered by our ambivalent allies. They may not bring you wealth, but they will trigger sync.

What is important to remember is that these entities are not really your friends. Jesus may be your homeboy and mommy Gaia may love you no matter what, but the beings of the crossroads are ambivalent; they are capricious. The combination of modern service culture and the Judaeo-Christian idea of a personal creator have given rise to some fairly alarming errors in magical thinking. Many of us have some unthinking expectation that the entire spiritual world exists to help you get that new iPad or 2 percent pay rise. The balance of evidence and the last fifty thousand years of human history suggests this is probably not the case.

The Trickster and Your Cosmology

If there is not a trickster in your personal cosmology, it is of limited psychological use to you and probably a bit unbalanced for the purposes of practical enchantment.

---

53   Carroll, *The Octavo*.

Typically these beings are found at the crossroads, so look there first. Even some aspects of Hekate fulfil this function, for instance. She is associated with crossroads, as well as Hermes. The fact that she predates the rest of the Olympian pantheon means she is not bound by the diktats of Zeus. (Recall the same notion of predating exists among the Winnebago and Iberian folk magicians.)

Religion in general does not overly interest the jobbing sorcerer. Indeed, the historical evidence suggests that they largely fitted into whatever dominant belief system was knocking around at the time, focusing more on acquiring and using practical techniques. Modern magic has confused classical relationships with the gods based on available archaeological evidence ... which necessarily favours "high church" relationships because such evidence is much more likely to survive. We look at Delphi or the Pantheon and discern either priestly or royal approaches to the divine, but they tell us little about how the wider populace behaved. The scant pieces of the common approach to the gods suggest an entirely different, low-tech, more transactional relationship. A similar ethos informs this book. We are not here to found a sci-fi religion or roleplaying circle. Pick an ambivalent ally and move on.

Here are some suggestions to get you started.

The Devil at the Crossroads

For centuries, the devil has fulfilled the role of trickster in the western tradition. Our expectation that he is some terrifying monster determined to destroy or rule the earth is a recent, cinematic creation. In early modern Europe he was certainly unpredictable but still entirely under the control of God—just as everything else was. He was bothersome rather than evil, like a friend who drinks too much or that neighbourhood cat who keeps getting into the house somehow.

The core "sin" that arose from association with the devil was idolatry, not soul loss or recruitment into the armies of hell. Thus, throwing votive objects in an old holy well became associating with the devil because of the inherent idolatry in believing that the well had capacities God could or would not fulfil.

In the New World in particular, the phrase "deal with the devil" became a sort of catch-all for any agreement undertaken between a human and the spirit world. Perhaps the most famous example of this is early blues singer-songwriter Robert Johnson, who took his guitar to the crossroads and played several evenings in a row. Eventually a "large, black man" showed up, tuned his guitar, and handed it back. For the rest of his short life, Johnson was an undisputed musical master. He spoke quite openly about his deal with the devil, but the consensus opinion appears to be that his actual agreement was with the loa ... probably Legba in particular.

If that is your road, you do not need me to show it to you. For the rest of us, it strikes me as about time we reopened this route. The crossroad ritual below calls on Lucifer rather than "the devil." There are a number of reasons for this. Firstly, the "devil" is something of a semantic moving target. Sometimes it *is* Lucifer, often it is a lot more. Lucifer's pre-Christian origins associate him with the planet Venus, the morning star (and/or evening star); thus he presides over liminal, crepuscular times—dawn or dusk. There is also his later Promethean associations in bringing light to earth; he brings things from the unmanifest to the manifest. (If you are still a little uncomfortable, recall that Jesus is also called "Morning Star." Figure that one out!)

STEP 1

The first step is obviously finding a quiet crossroad where you can be alone for several evenings. It is easier said than done if you live in West London, as I do. (The first time I performed a variant of this rite was in some tidal bushland on Sydney's Parramatta River. Much quieter.) You will need to return several nights in a row, so factor that in.

Step 2

On the first evening, write the following square on a piece of reasonably robust card. Remember, it can rain!

```
L U C I F E R
U N A N I M E
C A T O N I F
I N O N O N I
F I N O T A C
E M I N A N U
R E F I C U L
```

Go to the crossroads, conceal this square somewhere it will not be found or otherwise disturbed, clap your hands three times, and call out to Lucifer and say you wish to speak with him. Then walk away WITHOUT LOOKING BACK.

Step 3

The next part is quite variable. On successive nights, go to the crossroads and *feel*. There is no need to repeat the invocation (unless you determine that there is), merely hold the intention of contact in your head. Eventually there will be a sensation of awareness or expectation. If it is not there, come back again the next night. I appreciate this may be nonstandard procedure for those of you with some magical experience, but the goal here is to calibrate the crossroads for your reality... and his.

Step 4

One night, the presence will be unmistakable. Then, rub your hands with some of the dirt from the crossroads and say the following. (Have it written down beforehand.)

Lucifer, Ouyar, Chameron, Aliseon, Mandousin, Premy, Oriet,
Naydru, Esmony, Eparinesont, Estiot, Dumosson, Danochar,
Casmiel, Hayras, Fabelleonthu, Sodirno, Peatham, Venite, Venite,
Lucifer, Amen.[54]

At this point, speak aloud about why you are here, what you intend to get out of this arrangement and what you are willing to offer in return. Offerings include food, alcohol, praise, artwork dedicated to the spirit, and so on. You certainly do not need to offer your soul. (The fact that you are reading a magic book suggests its resale value is a lot lower than you probably think, anyway.)

When you have completed your exchange, thank the spirit for attendance and once again walk away without turning back.

Final Note

If you are more comfortable with "the devil" as a specific being rather than Lucifer, omit the magic square and the invocation. Clap and summon each night until you experience a change in the feel of the crossroads.

It is also worth noting that you now have yourself a power place for the regular leaving of offerings, quiet celebrations, or discussions with a spirit of the crossroads. These relationships build over time. You will get nowhere in magic or in life without a robust relationship with the Lord of the Crossroads in one form or another. Do not be a stranger; remember what I said about "ambivalence."

Hermes and Hermanubis

In terms of liminal, transgressive trickster allies, do not forget there are some reasonably extensive techniques for reaching Hermanubis in the previous chapter. He can certainly fulfill this role, too. I tend to call

---

54 Jake Stratton-Kent. *The True Grimoire*. Scarlet Imprint, 2009.

Hermanubis exclusively for necromancy but only because it is how my personal practice has evolved; the rule is far from universal.

As for Hermes/Mercury, there are any number of resources out there for achieving contact. Begin with classical sources and hymns. In either case, a small statue of Saint Christopher provides a subtle, suitable home for these beings (and will not alarm house guests quite so much as a statue of the devil!).

Other Allies

There is something quite crude about trying to fit overviews of gods into one or two chapters of occult books. If divine concepts could so easily be apprehended then there would be no need for occult books in the first place. It becomes even more difficult when attempting to convey some notion of Trickster beings or those that preside over High Strangeness and synchronicity.

As such, the following beings are representative. Much can be gained from further study of any or all of them. Not everything you read about needs to end up on your altar.

- Anansi
- Our Lady of Fatima
- Manu
- Loki
- Rabbit

Families Are Always Rising and Falling in America

The single biggest cause of bankruptcy in the United States is a bad health diagnosis. Our cognitive error in mistaking the postwar decades for "normal" means we have largely forgotten that Fortune, as a force or a goddess, brings both the good and the bad. The historical record is filled with hymns and spells to propitiate this being, to ensure that she brings good fortune rather than ill. In fact, the early church found this practice among the most difficult to erase. She was treated as a separate being—you could almost say *worshipped*——right through until the early modern period. Our ancestors were evidently prepared to tolerate a change of religious regime, but they were not stupid enough to leave Fortune unappeased for long. Words to live by.

There is much equanimity, wisdom, and insight to be gained through meditating on this personification of probability. Always, always have a go-to propitiation for Fortune/Isis Fortuna/Tyche, etc. I use a comparatively simple Orphic hymn to Tyche performed with the use of a chaplet; a kind of mini rosary blessed by the Pope, no less. (Long story.) Because every enchantment in this book has been personally, thoroughly road-tested over a number of years, I have to tell you that the ritual as it stands requires the Johns Hopkins University Press translation of the *Orphic Hymns*.[55] As other writers have found, this publisher is somewhat challenging to get quote clearances out of, so you will have to seek out the full version yourselves. (I suggest from a library.) In the interim, there are some excellent classical mentions and invocations found on the extensive theoi.com that may provide a stand-in. But a ritual is more than a random assortment of words and funny smells, so I will not do you the disservice of simply making up a hymn while carrying on with a different one in my personal practice.

Once you have sourced a satisfactory invocation or hymn to Tyche, simply light some frankincense incense, and if performing this outside, dig a small hole in the ground and pour in milk, honey, and wine. Repeat for each bead of the chaplet.

Like so much magic, you can really only tell if it is working *when* it is working. Expect curious synchronicities and chance encounters on the way to your goals. The general idea is to position yourself somewhere

---

55   Apostolos N. Athanassakis and Benjamin J. Wolkow, translators. *The Orphic Hymns*. Johns Hopkins University Press, 2013.

where there are greater probabilistic ranges of outcomes and find an ally who will help more than hinder you. Call it the portfolio strategy of religion: you just need to win slightly more often than you lose.

As for identifying potential losses, that is the subject of the next chapter.

THE MAGNIFICENT
GAME OF THE KING

One of the most interesting findings of precognition and presentiment
research is that people seem to be influenced by themselves in the
future, rather than by objective events. Precognitions are like memories
of the future. Presentiments seem to involve a physiological back-
flowing from future states of alarm or arousal, a flow of causation
moving in the opposite direction to energetic causation.

THE SCIENCE DELUSION, DR. RUPERT SHELDRAKE

Dedicated to the most powerful woman on earth at the time—Catherine
de Médici; the Florentine princess who became queen of France—a book
appeared in Bologna in 1551. It was called *One Hundred Liberal and In-
genious Games* and contained rules and instructions for various dice and
card games, both of which were extremely popular in northern Italy. One
was listed as the Magnificent Game of the King, wherein the four suits of

the traditional Italian playing cards represented the four cardinal virtues of prudence, justice, temperance, and fortitude. Here was a game that was also *more* than a game. It was a pastime that told the players something about the wider universe.

In what is a mildly amusing circular metaphor, precisely dating when the tarot appeared in Europe is something of a Fool's errand. Western esotericism's current views of the tarot are shaped more by late-eighteenth- and early-nineteenth-century French mystics seeking to tie everything back to Egypt. (This was easier to do in a time before hieroglyphs had been translated.) Subsequent Victorian occultists then overlaid Christian kabbalistic concepts and the Hebrew alphabet over the astrological correlations developed by their French predecessors. Whilst this is a pleasingly coherent system—reaching its apogee with Aleister Crowley's *Book of Thoth*—it lacks any historical veracity further back than its creators.

The broad consensus appears to be that card games had arrived in central and southern Europe by the 1300s from the Near East, if the admonitions of various holy men at the time are anything to go by. These games typical had four suits including mirrors, acorns, swords, and plants but had yet to coalesce into today's recognisable set of playing cards. Different regions had different variants and it was only later that the trump cards were added. (Early trumps contained a female pope which is now the High Priestess, and much of the religious concern about the cards may have sprung from this blasphemy.) These trumps appear to be based on the popular medieval mystery and morality plays that travelled Europe promoting Catholic and biblical eschatology to a mostly illiterate populace. Paul Huson, in his excellent *Mystical Origins of the Tarot*, suggests that the presence of Death in the trumps, as well as the general movement of the trump story from the physical to the metaphysical may have served as a *memento mori* for the wealthy of Europe when it was being ravaged by the Plague. In any case, the imagery that would have been instantly understood by the medieval mind became obscure and "mystified" only a few centuries later as the Renaissance blew away what it saw as the cobwebs of the ignorant worldview of the Dark Ages.

Sortilege—from the Latin *sortilegium*—as opposed to cartomancy has been around since mankind developed toolmaking capabilities. Dating back to the rise of Christianity, cards were used to generate random numbers referring to phrases in the Bible, Virgil, or Homer, for instance. So we have two behavioural streams, gaming and divination, coming down to us from the distant past in a way that is now impossible to disentangle.

And why would we want to? As we saw in the probability chapter, a mathematical understanding of risk and probable outcomes is an extremely late development. The difference between a game and a forecast was far less defined for our ancestors than it is for us. Both dealt with a future event that, at the time, was entirely out of your hands and in the hands of Fortune. ("Oh, I am Fortune's Fool!") Would she favour you or no? Thus we find ourselves once again in the realm of the trickster, in that liminal space between what is real and what is a game. Divination in general and cartomancy in particular can only ever have emerged in an environment of illegal tavern games, marginal cultures and forgotten fears of Plague death. Those eighteenth-century French occultists were correct in saying that the tarot contains the highest secrets of magic, just not in the way they thought.

The Science of the Magnificent Game

Along with telepathy, precognition is the most studied and most common psi effect. Over a century's worth of data has been generated in laboratory conditions on which we can draw. As Dr. Russell Targ says, from a statistical perspective the evidence for telepathy and precognition is ten times greater than the evidence that aspirin prevents heart attacks.

Getting your head around precognition and getting good at divination are probably the two steps you can take to magically improve your life over any other. Cartomancy has managed to accrete several centuries of mythology and folklore, much of which is unhelpful if you are in the business of, you know, getting an *accurate* view of likely outcomes. The fastest way to burn off these accretions is to hold them to the light of precognition's scientific and psychological evidence as well as their subsequent implications.

Firstly and most importantly, what is the most common form of precognition? For this, we must return to Cambridge biologist and personal hero Dr. Rupert Sheldrake in his *Science Delusion*.

> *On my database there are 842 cases of human premonitions, precognitions, or presentiments. Of these, 70 per cent are about dangers, disasters, or deaths; 25 per cent are about neutral events; and only five per cent are of happy events, like meeting a future spouse, or winning a raffle. Dangers, deaths and catastrophes predominate. This agrees with a survey of well-authenticated cases of precognition collected by the Society for Psychical Research in which 60 per cent concerned deaths or accidents. Very few were of happy events. Most of the others were trivial or neutral, although some were very unusual. In one such case, the wife of the Bishop of Hereford dreamed that she was reading the morning prayers in the hall of the Bishop's Palace. After doing so, on entering the dining room, she saw an enormous pig standing beside the table. This dream amused her, and she told it to her children and their governess. She then went into the dining room and an escaped pig was standing in the exact spot where she had seen it in her dream.*[56]

Right away you can see that these data are highly instructive. The first thing that leaps to mind is that the evidence for successful precognition comes from the complete opposite end of the question spectrum to what diviners commonly ask. Divination tends toward positive questions:

---

56   Rupert Sheldrake, *The Science Delusion*. Coronet, 2012.

"Where is my soul mate?" "How can I make more money?" Indeed, it is a common topic of discussion among professional tarot readers whether to sugarcoat negative readings and by how much.

It appears that precognitive accuracy increases when it comes to avoiding negative outcomes to possible actions. We may speculate a mechanism for understanding this: a future state of discomfort may be easier for our consciousness to detect in the present than a future state of comfort as they are not only more rare, but as Duke University's Dan Ariely's research demonstrates, humans are more concerned with avoiding negative outcomes than seeking positive ones regardless of the probabilities involved. There is potentially a very real opportunity to use our own cognitive biases to genuine advantage here in ways that have so far been under-explored.

Positive or negative, it seems that having a fixed outcome at the time of divination works better than having an indeterminate one. Here is Peter J. Carroll again, from his classic essay "Magical Theory":

> *When the magician divines he interacts primarily with future versions of himself. In divination he basically taps into what he may know in the future. A curious circularity seems to exist in divination; it only seems to work if at some point in the future you will end up knowing the result by ordinary means. This explains why the best results in divination seem to occur for either very short term divinations about unlikely things that will happen in the next few seconds, or for events which are heavily deterministic, but not yet obvious, in the further future.*[57]

Carroll's observations align with the findings of the notorious Stargate program; a NASA- and CIA-funded series of experiments into remote viewing that lasted for more than twenty years. Beginning during the height of the Cold War, the project successfully located down Soviet aircraft in the

---

57   Peter J. Carroll. "Magical Theory." Accessed April 12, 2015. www.specularium .org/wizardry/item/114-magical-theory.

jungles of Africa, kidnapping victims, the rings of Jupiter (before Voyager had been verified them), and dozens more. Over the course of its existence, the findings from thousands of experiments led to the development of some fairly robust protocols designed to maximise the accuracy of a remote viewing session. Most pertinent to classic divination are the following two:

Firstly, what is known as "feedback": the remote viewer is told whether the information he or she gave—and specifically which parts of it—were accurate or ultimately useful in achieving the objective, i.e., was the plane eventually found or not? This is functionally equivalent to divining for a fixed event in the future whose outcome you will eventually know. Not only does providing feedback improve the accuracy of the individual session, it *improves the overall accuracy of the viewer over time*. If you want to get better at divination—and who doesn't?—keep this in mind. Providing feedback is lifting barbells.

Secondly, contemporary magicians should consider what is known as "analytical overlay." A term coined by the Stargate Program's most successful remote viewier, Ingo Swann, it refers to the mind's natural tendency to interpret the imagery it is receiving *as it is receiving it*. Interpretation appears to require using a different part of the mind to precognition. Attempting interpretation during the precognitive part of a session leads to the imposition—the overlay—of the reader's personal opinions of what are going on rather than the clearest possible view of a future event. This rather defeats the purpose of divination, of course. If you want your own *opinion* of what is going to happen in the future, just put down the cards and ask yourself. From personal experience cartomancy has an inbuilt capacity to short-circuit analytical overlay. As long as you merely look at the images on the cards as you turn them over and resist leaping to an interpretation until you have overturned them all, you largely avoid getting in your own way.

Finally, and proving that my own lack of fashionability extends far beyond my wardrobe (don't judge, I'm not the one reading a chaos magic book!), is the classic notion of oblique strategies. It is perhaps a bit disingenuous to include it under a subheading that contains the word "science," smelling faintly as it does of smile therapy, fondue parties, and other long-since-dismissed concepts from the seventies, oblique strategies are nevertheless highly instructive for the improved performance of cartomancy, particularly for beginners. The general idea, so deliciously and repeatedly skewered in the 1991 film *Slacker*, is that randomised and typically counterintuitive suggestions can lead to breakthroughs in creative thinking'.

Whether that is applicable to your own life or no, there is much to be gained even from what would otherwise be considered failed divinations—i.e., predictions that subsequently prove to be in error. Consider an individual tarot reading to be a brainstorming session for one. Typically the magician does not resort to divination except in situations where he or she is stuck or unaware of the best course of action. Often the layout or interpretation of the cards will suggest an approach that can unstick the magician regardless of whether the reading was accurate or not.

In these situations, note the prediction nonetheless (for feedback, yeah?) but lend more credence to the unsticking suggestion that has just appeared in your mind. A big part of this approach is "giving yourself permission" (for want of a less annoying term) to experiment with the form of cartomancy. You otherwise run the risk of frontloading your mind with outcome-anxiety and missing the session's most valuable component. Unless your life goal is to become the world's most gifted psychic, what you actually want from a divination is not to envision your preferred outcome, but to actually *get to it*.

Forecasting

So it would seem that the human capacity for precognition is better used in avoiding negative outcomes, and it appears that the probabilistic nature of reality makes the likelihood of predictive accuracy *diminish* the further into the future the querent looks, especially in cases where feedback is unlikely.

How are we to cohere these consciousness effects into a workable predictive system for generating preferred life outcomes, especially where it comes to wealth? Enter monthly forecasting.

Astrology

Astrology is a bit like hairdressing. Not only is it likely you will have to admit defeat and visit an expert rather than attempt it yourself, it can take a while to find one who doesn't make you look like a just-escaped mental patient. When you do find one, cleave to him or her for as long as you can.

Even if you consider astrology to be little more than a randomised correlation between seven common topics and the perspective error that gives humans the impression that our nearest stellar bodies appear to move regularly through the earth's night sky—which is perfectly reasonable, by the way—as a sort of checklist for regular divinatory subjects, it works better than most other systems.

As to astrology's predictive efficacy, I will just highlight in passing that the *one* time CSICOP—the so-called Committee for the Scientific Investigation into Claims of the Paranormal—actually *did* some scientific investigation, it was into the predictive power of natal charts correlated with sporting prowess. They found a (small) correlation that led to resignations and claims of falsifying data in an attempt to prove no correlation.[58] They stopped investigating and have spent the past forty years shouting from the sidelines instead. The group actually completely dropped "scientific investigation" from its name in 2006. The more you know, eh?

Even something as vanilla as a monthly sun sign horoscope can provide the catalyst for an improved monthly forecast. For example, in addition to a broad divination such as "What are the top challenges facing me in the month of May?" one can add:

---

58   Chris Carter. *Science and Psychic Phenomena: The Fall of the House of Skeptics.* Inner Traditions, 2012.

- I wish to know more about the potential conflict with a work colleague.
- What is behind the arguments I am having with my partner?
- I wish to know more about my chest problems.

You will note that these questions, while not specifically *negative* in and of themselves, give the diviner a wider context for looming challenges. They also very much leave the door open for full feedback. Whether it "works" in any objective sense, astrology can indicate those Rumsfeldian "known unknowns" that may otherwise slip by.

Monthly Reporting

Much of this procedure can be performed on a smartphone. I actually do most of it on the bus on the way to work the morning my monthly horoscope is published online. I read Susan Miller's astrologyzone.com, but you may be after a different hair style.

Firstly, start a Google doc or similar that will be used for your monthly forecast. Over time you will end up with a reverse chronology of the year. Then make some notes under the following headings.

- **You:** Bullet point your thoughts, opinions, milestones, unexamined predictions for the calendar month. This is not a clairvoyant exercise—it is almost the complete opposite, in fact. Start with this one because it can serve as your control group for the other systems of forecasting. You basically want to jot down your unassisted guess of what the next month has in store for you. Then you want to *completely* push it out of your mind. Genuinely visualise an icon of scrunched paper landing in a wastebasket, that sort of thing.
- **The stars:** Summarise the points that seem pertinent from your monthly horoscope. Incidentally, you will be mostly

wrong as to which points seem relevant at the beginning of the month. Then hopefully the next month you will be a little less wrong, and so on as time goes on. (Such is the theory, anyway.)

- **The cards:** Bullet point the pertinent points from a monthly tarot reading as described above. If you have a smartphone, take a photo of the spread because just as with the horoscope, the parts that seem pertinent at the beginning of the month will seem less so at the end.

Only once this is done should you read over the previous month. Consider it your feedback.

Nothing in the monthly forecast precludes doing situation-specific divination. If anything, it helps to correlate which parts of your life may require either a little divinatory or sorcerous assistance, but it is a supremely helpful baseline. Some entirely new perspectives emerge when you begin with your *opinion* of what will happen that month and then layer over several different divinatory system. A few friends include a monthly geomantic reading as well, apparently to great effect. Whichever layers you choose, the aim is to frontrun the universe as much as possible.

Cartomancy

Technically, you can use any sufficiently complex system of divination that takes your fancy. These can include runes, geomancy, or the I Ching.

But let me tell you something about me. If you couldn't tell from the introduction to this chapter, I love the tarot. Love it. Not just tarot either, but pretty much any form of cartomancy. I have dozens of decks. Some are worn and filthy from more than two decades of magical campaigns, and others are unbelievably expensive and too precious to use regularly. (For instance, a hand-printed Sibilla Oracle I got from one of the few remaining original printers in Florence ... a city that was famous for magic, cartomancy, and printing for centuries.)

Never let anyone tell you that you cannot buy your own cards, that you cannot read for yourself, that only amateurs use the accompanying interpretations, that only some tarot systems are valid, that you should never read for people you know, or that you should never read when you are unwell. Humans have been divining for at least thirty thousand years and we are still working out the rules. These objects need to interface with *your* consciousness, after all, and you will always be the supreme expert in that particular field.

Why and Which Tarot?

Why tarot, specifically, rather than any other system of cartomancy? Well, this is a bit glib, but a game based on medieval courtly life filled with pitfalls and deception, zero opportunity for upward mobility that isn't assigned via destiny where you begin with absolutely nothing and *hopefully* end with nothing more than a good death more closely matches today's economic situation than I think most of us would care to admit.

As for which decks, let me immediately contradict myself regarding listening to other people's tarot advice and suggest, humbly, that beginners select tarot decks that have images and clear meaning descriptions on *each* card rather than just the trumps and the court cards. At the very least, this leads to quicker and possibly more efficient meaning recall.

The second consideration is to ensure that if you are selecting a themed deck it has sufficient emotional range. I have several tarot decks on the theme of Arthurian mythology and the Grail cycle, for instance. These stories have a sufficient amount of sex, death, misfortune, and triumph to be able to speak the nonlinguistic language of the unconscious. "The Flowers of West Wales Tarot" probably does not. You are effectively teaching your mind to speak to itself in images like a zoologist would with a depressed gorilla or precocious dolphin.

Calibration

There is an element of that Christmas morning feeling when one receives a new tarot deck. Typically the cards are pulled out, looked through, briefly shuffled, and then taken for their first road test. This is fine; it is your money and they are your cards after all. The next step, however, really should be working out which combination of image and meaning matches your own interpretation and unconscious. This process is called calibration.

Begin with the deck and accompanying book sitting beside you. Lift the first card and see if you can discern its traditional meaning. Check the book to see if you are correct. If you *are* correct, place this card to the left of the main pile and to the right if you are not. Move on to the next card.

Continue the process until you have exhausted the main deck leaving you with two piles, one of cards whose meanings you recall and one whose meanings you do not. Shuffling the pile of cards whose meanings escaped you on the first round and repeat, checking each meaning against the book as you go.

Eventually—in less time than it appears when written out like this—you will have a full deck of cards whose meanings you know. At this point, shuffle and run through them one more time, then put them away for the rest of the day. Interleaving or interleaved practice is a method of studying used as a memory recall booster. Rather than cramming, recall is higher in instances where there are gaps in study or memorisation.

By no means does calibration imply that book interpretations are the only valid ones. Instead, consider it like learning your ABCs before you can begin to read and write. Similarly, it does not imply that you cannot begin using your cards until you have memorised their meanings … this is akin to memorising music rather than learning how to read it—you are trying to squish the wrong thing into your mind. It is impossible. Each sitting and each querent will be different. Personally, I can barely remember all my email passwords; I would have no chance of memorising each and every meaning of each and every card of each and every deck. Consult the book regularly and unashamedly. Many of my favourite companion volumes are of such a high standard of research that they function as independent sources of insight anyway.

Nested Divination

When you have multiple card sets and use them regularly, certain characteristics, shortcomings, and areas of expertise become apparent. Just as there are different golf clubs for different shots, you will discover that certain oracles are better suited to specific situations. For example, my Sibilla oracles are deeply paranoid, concerned with surprise visitors, double-dealing business associates, family members with their own agendas, illicit love affairs, that sort of thing. As such, they make excellent "classic fortune telling" decks because they deal with mundane issues that would lead you to the proverbial gypsy wagon parked at the edge of the town fair one evening (assuming you lived in a racist cartoon/Cher music video).

Other decks deal with loftier or at least larger issues to do with personal destiny, life goals, and the wider movements of fate that are more likely to mark cornerstones in your incarnation. Then there are either the "darker" decks whose "good" cards aren't actually all that good and their interminable opposite, the lighter oracles where even a cancer diagnosis is presented with an abundance of kittens.

You will only find out the limits of your oracles' emotional ranges by pushing past them and throwing a really bad or inappropriate spread. The good news is this tends to only happen once. After that, you begin to develop an appreciation for which oracles work best in each situation. And *that* allows you to do something really quite neat. *Comme ça*:

In situations where a card spread—typically one thrown using your most-used set—surfaces a card that you know has a very specific meaning such as malicious office gossip or family health problems you can "jump" up or down into another oracle system that is better matched to the challenge. The classic advice is to pull a few additional cards for clarity from the deck you are currently using, but this strikes me as asking the universe to type you up a new letter after you have removed at least ten keys from the keyboard. (The keys being the cards that are already laid out in the spread. What if they are needed for the clarifying message?) Granted, this is a bit unwieldy for a professional card reader (although I have certainly seen it done), but the focus of this book is *you*. Take your time, get the best reading.

As for which specific spreads to use, concerns regarding space and also a general pointlessness in doing so leave little time for their discussion. Each deck worth its salt will come with variations of classic spreads such as the Celtic Cross or three-card spread, and the Internet abounds with thousands of more suggestions. If the images on the cards are the letters forming the words your unconscious uses to speak, the spread is the grammar that builds the sentences. The process of spread discovery is as unique as meaning discovery.

Cartomantic Ritual

By now it should be fairly obvious that with such a long and enigmatic history, the notion that there is one right way to perform cartomancy is balderdash. However the notion that one should demarcate the cards and the space in which they are used as separate from everyday life is pretty close to universal. This can be as simple as visualising them bathed in a blinding white light that removes all previous energetic imprints.

Another option, one with a little more drama, is inspired by the western Iberian folk tradition of calling on Saint Zachariah for acts of divination and fortune telling, by way of *the Book of St Cyprian: The Sorcerer's Treasure*. In the Biblical legend, Zachariah was the temple priest who, in his old age, received a message from Gabriel that he and his barren wife would give birth to John the Baptist. He is struck dumb as a result of his disbelief of the angel's message until the day the child is born and named. As such, he is related to notions of spirit communication, prophecy, and its fulfilment on earth. The eagle-eyed mythographers among you will also spy that this particular saint and invocation folds back into the Headless Rite earlier in the book by virtue of the connection between Zachariah and John the Baptist. (Stick with me, baby. Oh, the places you'll go!)

Consecration

STEP 1
Gather some incense, even a joss stick will do, and have the cards to hand.

STEP 2
Recite the following as you light the incense:

> *May the merciful God enter the Holy Place and*
> *accept with favour the offering of his people.*

For context, in the vanishingly unlikely scenario in which Zachariah was a historical person, this is the best guess as to the prayer he would have recited in the temple just prior to Gabriel's appearance. But events do not need to have happened in the physical for them to drip with power and utility.

STEP 3
Wave the cards through the smoke and say:

> *Most holy Saint Zachariah*
> *Thou wert deaf and mute,*
> *Thou had a son*
> *And thou called him John,*
> *Declare to me the true prophecies of heaven*
> *through the medium of these cards.*
>
> *With the permission of IAO SABAOTH,*
> *Amen.*

That's it for consecration. Any time afterward when you wish to use your cards you can either recite the Zachariah prayer or simply call on him to reveal the prophecies/will of heaven.

Conclusion

Divination, in conjunction with enchantment, form practical sorcery's one-two punch. From a strictly chaos magic perspective, the available data suggest that one should always enchant long and divine short. Our consciousness seems better built to spy future negative events whilst simultaneously preferring to assume positive outcomes are more likely to occur. It also appears to be significantly better at *predicting* future events than changing them.

Thus we arrive at an inevitable extension to chaos magic's classic axiom, especially when it comes to wealth and success magic. Enchant long for positive outcomes and divine short to avoid negative ones.

The data also suggest, paraphrasing Russell Targ, that if you do not commonly dream of airplane crashes but have one the night before you are due to fly, you are better off skipping the flight than attempting to change the outcome with magic. When it comes to getting the seat with extra legroom, however, I have something else in mind.

WISH GRANTING
SQUIGGLES

Magic works in practice but not in theory.

PETER J. CARROLL

If you have picked up this book for reasons other than familiarity with my blog, *Rune Soup*, then I should probably tell you that sigils are its accidental *spécialité de la maison*. If you have picked up the book because you *are* familiar with my blog, then this is likely the chapter you skipped to while standing in the store. Buy the damn book already.

For better or for worse, sigil magic has come to be seen as the defining technique of the chaos system. For much of my magical career, I wasn't that interested in it. Firstly, the most famous—but by no means only—method of sigil activation involved masturbation and this seemed to my teenage mind to be a waste of a good wank. (If I only had time for five or six a day, why spend one on magic?) Secondly, I had sunk all this money into pendants and wands and incense and trinkets—*you* try getting High John the Conquerer in regional Australia pre-Internet—so why would I put all that effort aside for just pen and paper? It seemed so unwizardly.

The thread running through my misconceptions was probably due to a personal failure to consider sigil magic in its wider historical context—a failure that remains visible in the occult world to this day. We shall endeavour to correct that by beginning—inevitably—at the beginning.

Leaving aside their myriad ways of construction and enchantment, what a sigil ultimately "is" is a pictographic representation of an idea or outcome. There are repeating patterns of red ochre paint found in caves in southern Africa that are one hundred millennia old, giving us our earliest known evidence of what is called symbolic thinking... which means having one thing represent something else. On the surface, that may sound like a simplistic development, but it is *the* original act of sorcery from which all others come and is as good a point as any from which to date the emergence of humans into full consciousness. Having a thing stand in for another thing is a deliberate act of creation that is exceedingly rare. The Pacific octopus may be highly intelligent and possessed of its own language of body movements and pigment changes, but they don't tend to write too many off-Broadway shows. (I would spend more time at the theatre if they did!)

Thus sigil magic techniques as most commonly found in chaos magic are a direct continuation of that first act of sorcery. They have been rendered down and had the intervening thousands and thousands and thousands of years—the hieroglyphs of Egypt, the defixiones of Rome, the seals of the grimoire spirits, the symbols of the planets—cooked off, leaving only the magician and his or her symbolic capacity. In many ways it is an outrageous act of vandalism and probably one of the main reasons why sigil magic—and chaos magic—remain so persistently unpopular in the wider occult discourse.

Unpopular though it may be, it possesses a huge advantage over any other form of popular enchantment: iteration speed. It was the realisation of this advantage that triggered my come-to-Jesus with sigil magic and led to—may I humbly submit—my own contribution to its ongoing canon. Let me explain what I mean by iteration speed.

In 1959, British Industrialist Henry Kremer founded the eponymous Kremer Prize, administered by the Royal Aeronautical Society, which continues to this day (there are two prizes remaining). The first two prizes were both for human-powered flight: one for the first machine that could fly a figure-of-eight between two markers a half-mile apart and the second for one that could cross the English Channel. More than a decade of failed attempts went by before a would-be competitor named Paul Mac-Cready turned his mind to the challenge. MacCready realised that the problem that needed to be solved was *not* human-powered flight. The problem was that no one understood the problem. Previous applicants would spend up to a year building a flying machine only to have it fail and send them quite literally back to the drawing board. The speed of learning was too slow. Other applicants were not building on enough new data in between their attempts. MacCready discovered that the real challenge that needed solving was one of iteration speed: how to build a machine that could attempt flight, fail and *be quickly modified to try again*. Pursuing a big goal in large, single attempts—with only a limited understanding of all the intervening complexities—was not going to get the job done fast enough. So MacCready solved a different problem: how can you design a flying machine that can be rebuilt in hours instead of weeks or months? He and his team went on to solve this challenge and in the late seventies won both the figure-of-eight prize and the English Channel prize, netting the equivalent of $3.8 million in today's money.

In the modern world, whether you achieve your goals or not depends on how you navigate the intervening complexity between where you are and where you want to be. Processes and outcomes have become infinitely more complicated. In previous eras you would enchant for a good harvest, a largely binary event over which you have minimal intervening control (hence recourse to sorcery). Getting yourself from the family home in the suburbs of Arizona to a super-yacht moored off a Croatian island or whatever your goal happens to be requires significantly more steps and a healthy appetite for iteration. Sigils often provide the best opportunity to solve the real problem.

Sigils and Psychology

As practiced today, sigil magic is a modification of a system created by Austin Osman Spare, a twentieth-century London occultist and only latterly celebrated artist. He was exploring some cutting-edge psychological theories that are now more than a century old and require revisiting. Spare's hypothesis was that all magic manifested via processes in the unconscious mind which only spoke the language of symbols and emotions. The conscious mind—possessed of language and artifice—merely got in the way. Thus the goal of magic was to *occupy* the conscious mind while sneaking a symbolic request into your unconscious where, left unmolested, it would eventually manifest. Once this was completed, the magician need only ensure they *never* recall their goal ever again because this would bring it back up from the unconscious into the conscious mind. Unless you are an alcoholic or suffer from a severe mental illness, this is functionally impossible... particularly if the goal is something like "money to buy food to feed my children." Your conscious mind has a tendency to notice when these kinds of goals go unfulfilled.

With the dubious benefit of an extra century of psychological and psychiatric research, Spare's operating hypothesis can be improved upon... although he should certainly be congratulated for getting more right than he did wrong. Firstly, the divide between the unconscious and the conscious is not nearly as clean-cut as Spare presumed. Many psychologists would go so far as to say it is an entirely illusory—albeit convenient—heuristic. The practical implication is that you will not break the world if you accidentally recall the goal of your enchantment. Indeed, the unencumbered movement of a concept up from your unconscious to your conscious and back again may even improve the likelihood that your enchantment will stick in the same way moving a visual or a fact in between your short- and long-term memory improves overall recall. I unashamedly offer you anecdotal evidence, from my own life no less, that this is indeed the case.

There is a caveat to that first point, and it is actually the entirety of the second point: when it comes to the unconscious only speaking the language of symbols, Spare was definitely onto something. His is a very well-corroborated hypothesis with supporting evidence from studies in sense memory, colour therapy, psychotherapy, neuroscience, as well as pretty much the entire history of art. For occultists, the most useful evidence comes from the kind of experiments into non-local consciousness effects we have encountered in previous chapters. When Dr. Russell Targ ran an experiment using remote viewing to correctly predict silver futures on the commodities exchange nine weeks in a row—making $120,000 and the front page of *the Wall Street Journal* in the process—he did not have his remote viewers attempt to predict the price swing directly.[59] Remote viewing, like all non-local consciousness effects, appears to work better with textures, shapes, and feelings than with numbers and letters. Instead, he got his viewers to describe the object the trader who actually made the silver trade for them would hand to him at the end of the week: a bottle of champagne if silver closed up a lot or a cold pancake if it closed down a lot.

The practical implications of this for magicians working principally via manipulation of their own consciousness is to put some effort into the aesthetics of your spellwork so as not to trigger an "ick" reaction from

---

59   Russel Targ. *The Reality of ESP: A Physicist's Proof of Psychic Abilities.* Quest Books, 2012.

your unconscious. Here's that word, again—find an *oblique* route to your goal...like a sigil.

In whatever tradition you belong to, there is much to be gained from the detailed study of these kinds of experiments. I am of the opinion that the most important magical research performed in the twentieth century happened outside the insular world of ceremonial magic and it has only been in the last decade or so that this has started to come to light. The surface remains almost entirely unscratched.

Classic Sigil Construction

Never in my life did I think I would be in a situation where I could quote myself (speaking of masturbation), but seeing as the post on *Rune Soup* in question has been viewed almost a quarter of a million times since publication, why attempt to catch lightning in a bottle twice?

——————

"Classic" is meant in the loosest possible sense, of course. What it really means is "post-Spare." There is no better introduction to classical sigil construction and chaos magic in general than Grant Morrison's late nineties gem, "Pop Magic."

Here is what you do:

- Write out your desire/goal
- Cross out all the vowels
- Cross out all the repeated letters

Mash the remaining letters into a single (hideous) glyph. Then start amending this glyph until it starts to look more pleasing. I try to make mine look organic or petroglyphic, but that's a personal preference. Your unconscious is different from mine. (Probably.)

You really can't get this wrong. Of course, you'll think you are doing it wrong the first few times. Common concerns include:

- "This still looks too much like the original letters."
- "This looks nothing like the original letters."
- "This doesn't look very 'magical.'"

Well, it doesn't need to *look like* anything. But it works better if it looks pleasing. And only you will know when you get to "pleasing."

There are some recommended changes to the classic copy construction I have picked up from years of hoodwinking people into buying things they probably don't need.

- Use positive words rather than negative words.
- Have fixed or clear goals.
- Use the present tense.
- Describe the completed situation rather than the desire to get there.

———

Those of you who are familiar with the piece will see my intention with this chapter is to fill in some of the background research and thinking that led to the creation of my sigil creation method. Ensuring your sigils look pleasing, for instance, is based on my interpretation of Stargate Program research suggesting that "enjoyable" and "unenjoyable" are easiest for the unconscious to recognise rather than a personal predisposition for pretty things.

If I were to take this book from your hands and start underlining parts of it, what is most important to keep in mind is using the present tense to describe completed situations. Examples would include "I am a size 8" rather than "It is my will to lose weight." You see how the latter encodes a

lack rather than a success. Using the "lose weight" sentence effectively en-
chants the desire to be on a diet rather than living at your goal weight!

And while we are at it please, *please* quit it with the "it is my will"
claptrap. The notion of will is a monumentally misunderstood Victorian atavism that bears no relation to what the previous century of personality and consciousness studies has given us. It makes you sound like
a stroppy, pompous toddler … and this is coming from a guy who just
quoted himself.

Shoaling and Probability

A shoal is a group of fish. When they all swim in the one direction, they are
schooling. When they are hanging out for reasons of safety, hydrodynamic
efficiency, and general social reasons, they are shoaling. Having grown up
in a house overlooking three beaches, been wreck and shark diving all over
the Pacific, shot a documentary on a sunken city, *and* previously worked for
Discovery Channel, using "shoal" as my group noun for sigils was probably
an inevitability.

The whole notion of launching multiple sigils at once emerged through
experimentation with complex magical targets. We presumably have fantasy fiction to thank for the belief that larger goals (more specifically, "lower
probability goals") require the input of larger amounts of sorcerous energy,
longer rituals, more expensive sacrifices, and so on. Such a belief, although
pleasingly dramatic, does not align very well with what we understand
about probability and the very real but *small* changes consciousness can
effect in the physical world. Pete Carroll describes our situation thusly in
The Octavo:

> *Daunting probabilites often appear for complex tasks like winning
> in war or business or love from a weak initial position; however all of
> those steps involved in winning may not actually look so impossible
> individually.*

The probability of throwing a dozen heads consecutively comes out at a desperate 0.000024, so only one person in four thousand might achieve it on average. However each individual step has a 0.5 probability and a magician with any sense will choose to attack such steps individually rather than go head to head against such formidable odds.[60]

Shoaling as a process came out of the realisation that achieving a big goal—such as complete financial independence—was best achieved through the successful eventuation of dozens of smaller, *higher probability* outcomes. Taking "financial independence" as a hypothetical example, these smaller components could include a promotion for your husband/wife/partner, the resignation of a colleague you are in competition with, improved visibility within your wider industry, improved physical health, and so on. After each successful shoal, the probabilistic "critical path" to the magician's big goal shifts and he or she reloads and goes again. Consider it the Kremer Prize approach to practical enchantment. If it were simply a matter of throwing more energy at a big problem, then not only would the Aztec civilisation still be around but you would not be reading this book because you would already be wealthy … or at least you would be reading it on the deck of your super-yacht in Croatia. Right away you see how shoaling works in concert with divination: divine for the pitfalls and shoal sigils to nudge for beneficial probabilistic outcomes that avoid or skirt around them. If I had to put the secret of my success such as it is into a single sentence, it would be the previous one.

The initial results of shoaling multiple sigils in the one activation session were orders of magnitude better than anticipated. Based on nothing but personal opinion, I attribute this to an inevitable reduction in lust of result. Recall that Spare believed that keeping your goal, your *need*, in your

---

60   Peter J. Carroll. *The Octavo.*

conscious mind while attempting to communicate it to the unconscious immediately scuppered your attempt. When you create five or six sigils to launch in the one sitting, it is much easier to consciously forget which particular sigil is encoded with which particular goal. To your eyes, they simply become wish granting squiggles.

With practice, shoaling also improves your magical target selection as you develop an intuitive understanding of the high and low probabilities of preferred outcomes in your life. For instance, if you are struggling with self-image issues, it may be better to enchant for a torrid, extramarital affair than a better haircut and wardrobe because the affair can only eventuate given five or six intervening preferred outcomes. Over time your improved capacity to assess probability and risk bleeds into other areas of your existence. This is the life's work of a chaos magician: fine-tuning probabilistic dials for fun and profit.

Robofish

Continuing my entirely arbitrary marine metaphors, we turn now to the robofish. The term comes from a 2010 University of Leeds study into fish behaviour. The researchers created a robot stickleback fish and placed it among some live sticklebacks. When the robofish made bold or fast moves, the other fish tended to follow it, providing insight into how shoals form and schools move … it appears that having the robofish behave in a decisive way makes the real fish think it knows something they do not, and so they follow suit.

Folding this idea into sigil magic, in every shoal be sure to include a sigil for an event that is happening or is guaranteed to happen, such as "I eat spaghetti tonight" or "I am in my house." This sigil is the robofish. In my personal experience, the improvement in preferred sorcerous outcomes is simply night and day. We may speculate some mechanism as to why this may be so. If we are in fact communicating requests to our unconscious, sending a simultaneous request for something that is completed or in the process of being completed with some goals that have yet to be completed may serve as a trigger of where—the physical—and *when*—the now—the results are expected. Indeed, it was seeking to improve the *when* that led my discovery of the robofish technique in the first place. I was looking for a way to hasten the arrival of my preferred outcomes which at the time were behaving far too much like standard shipping for my liking.

Sigil Activation

As should be evident by now, I am a proponent of the operating hypothesis that sigils work through some little-explored function of human consciousness (which is not to say I am exclusively a proponent of psychological models of magic). From a practical perspective, that means any suggestions as to how you can activate them will necessarily be limited because it is *your* unconscious, not mine, that we are seeking to influence.

There is a stereotypical image of a mid-nineties chaos magician spray-painting sigils in a post-industrial wasteland and a more updated stereotype of chaotes—horror of horrors—reblogging each other's sigils on tumblr. Experimental methods are fine as far as they go—which is often not very far, hence the need for experimentation—but if one is to take this technique seriously, a more stable and reliable launch procedure is required.

Firstly, you need a space that is dramatically and aesthetically pleasing. If you resonate with an eldritch, tentacled *mise-en-scène* then let that inform how you dress and prepare your ritual space. This is not an off-the-shelf consideration; it will be unique to you. My own preference is for a visual style I might call "South Pacific hoodoo" if I were in the mood to make the whole Internet angry at me. You can only get this wrong by overthinking it.

Step 1
Pre-Ritual Preparation
Typically I use any old pen and paper to generate the five or so sigils I intend to launch. Once I am happy with their designs, I inscribe each finalised

sigil on an individual piece of black card or art paper using a gold paint pen. Again, this is for aesthetic reasons. They look lovely in the low light of candles and incense smoke in a darkened room, as if they are positively *squirming* to get off the paper and into the ether. Definitely visit your nearest art supply store and pick out your own iteration of what "nice" sigils will look like to you. This will depend largely on your own artistic talent. Mine is nonexistent, hence the paint pen.

Once you have your finalised sigils, gather them with the candles, incense, lighters, and anything else you will need in your ritual space.

Step 2
RITUAL OPENING
It goes without saying that both you and the private space you are using are physically clean. (Or possibly deliberately dirty if you are going for a *Constantine* vibe.)

Lay out and light your candles and incense and arrange your sigil cards in front of you. Most often I do this sitting or squatting in front of a woven Fijian mat on the floor of my ritual space.

Close your eyes, turn a little to your right and sweep your hand in front of you, visualising grey dust and miasma being swept hundreds of feet away from you, through roofs and walls, as if blasted with a leaf blower, before ultimately dissolving. At the same time, say

HEKAS, HEKAS, ESTE BEBELOI

Continue around in a full circle, sweeping with your hand and repeating the phrase. Go round again if you feel the need. Return to/sit in front of your sigils and candles.

Step 3

INVOCATION

Every magician needs a magician's god or goddess. Find a being or beings in your preferred pantheon who are universally regarded for magical prowess. You do not need to select one based on rulership of your main goal; you need one who is all about the magic. We are creating a manifestation space here. Depending on the project and my headspace, my two go-to beings—at least when it comes to gods—are either Isis or the Abrahamic God (reached by aligning oneself with the super-powered folk saints and mythical personalities of the Old Testament).

Let us start with Isis. I regularly use an invocation based on an Isis aretalogy translated in the mid-twentieth century by the biblical scholar Frederick C. Grant. You can instantly find it online by looking for either "Cyme Inscription" or "Isis Aretalogy." Then it is a simple matter of replacing the repeated instances of "I am" with "thou art." Nevertheless, once again demonstrating the extreme disconnect between much of the legacy publishing and digital worlds, the copyright was more than difficult to track down so it won't appear in print here. Instead, I commend to you the opening lines of the *Ave Maris Stella*, first written in the sixth century, so we are probably fine on the copyright front. Whilst the debate regarding whether Mary is or is not Isis will have you up arguing till sunrise at Pagan parties, *Our Lady, Star of the Sea* is a fairly transparent borrowing of the Isis of the Late Period. For our purposes, the *Ave Maris Stella* plugs into the same current in a conveniently copyright-free way.

Ave Maris Stella.

Dei mater alma
Atque semper Virgo
Felix Cœli porta.

Sumens illud "Ave."

Gabrielis ore
Funda nos in pace,
Mutans Evæ nomen.

Solve vincla reis
Profer lumen cæcis
Mala nostra pelle
Bona cuncta posce.

Option B is the Petropolitanus Academicus invocation as translated by Ioannis Marathakis in his edition of the Hygromanteia. You do not need to use both invocations. In fact, you probably shouldn't.

> *Lord our God, Adouni, Elisabaoth, Lamekh, Sante, Lamantou,*
> *Khamatan, Tetragrammaton, Beginning and End; holy, holy, holy*
> *Lord Sabaoth, the whole heaven and earth are full of your glory;*
> *our father which art in heaven, uphold us with your holy names,*
> *holy Lord God Sabaoth; by the prayers of the holy forefathers*
> *Enos, Cainan, Mahalaleel, Methouselah, Seth, Enoch, Noah,*
> *Melchizedek, Joshua the son of Nun, Abraham, Isaac and Jacob,*
> *David and Jesse, Solomon and Rehoboam; by the prayers of yours*
> *saints, O Lord our God, be my saviour, merciful to me, my defender*
> *and my assistant. Amen.*[61]

Step 4
ACTIVATION

By now you should be in a mildly altered state of consciousness. Sit, relax some more, and look down at your sigils. This is a passive activation

---

61   Marathakis, Ioannis. *The Magical Treatise of Solomon, or Hygromanteia.* Golden Hoard Press, 2012.

method akin to a mandala meditation. Sit and breathe until you are ready to proceed.

Pick up each sigil card in turn and hold it a comfortable distance from your face. Stare at it. Do not rush. Just as in meditation, if your thoughts wander, gently bring them back to the form of the sigil. Look at it as if you are seeing it for the first time. Let your eyes unfocus so that its lines begin to warp and double.

After an indeterminate time, the sigil you are holding will... this is difficult to describe... *deflate*. The sensation will be as if the object you are holding was previously magical and has gone back to being inert, just a piece of card. When that happens, say the following phrase, put it down and pick up the next sigil.

Does not matter. Need not be.

Continue along this line until all your sigils have activated. Very occasionally you will find one that does not appear to resonate or refuses to "deflate." Put it down, pick up another one and return to it at the end of the launch. I have no explanation for why this happens, but it does.

Close as appropriate to whatever being you initially invoked.

Step 5
THE AFTERMATH

Austin Spare suggested destroying your sigils once they had been activated which is certainly an option for you if it feels appropriate. But there is a phenomenon I have encountered working in media and advertising known as "low attention processing." Essentially, it is when you are being advertised to without your conscious awareness that it is happening, and it is probably how most advertising works, as well as why so many ad execs drink so heavily. Even with a single, background exposure to an advertisement, brand preference increases. I know you are thinking this wouldn't

WISH GRANTING SQUIGGLES   141

happen to you, but everyone thinks that about advertising. That's called the "third person effect." (My people have words for everything.)

Instead of destroying your sigils, I recommend putting them up somewhere visible where they will quickly fade into the background of your daily life. For me this is typically on the mirror in the bedroom, or blu-tacked to a window you walk past every day. If low attention processing is a method of unconscious communication, we may as well attempt to utilise it. There is potentially an additional benefit to this approach which is that, eventually, you genuinely will completely forget what each of those sigils was for. I am looking at a few pasted up on the window in front of me and I *honestly* have no idea what they are about. These can be removed over time or at random.

One final note. Given that we do not really know the mechanism of action by which sigils actually work I am perhaps being overly superstitious, but using them for curse work or malefica is not recommended. There is a commonly understood psychological concept called priming whereby what you look at or experience influences your state of mind. So people who are exposed to words like "elderly," "retirement," and "hip replacement" when filling out surveys actually move slower and with more pain after completing the surveys than those who were not exposed to the same words. However it works, a vengeful or violent phrase, even in sigilised form, probably doesn't belong floating around in your own unconscious.

Further Implementation

As sigil magic is such a pared-down technique, it naturally lends itself to experimentation. One of the first ones to consider is further altering your consciousness when activating your sigils. A common manifestation of this is to turn your intention into a nonsensical mantra rather than an image via a similar process of removing repeating letters, vowels, and then shifting around what you have left over until it sounds right. Repetitions of the phrase then replace the visual activation method. An extension of this process would be to (legally) alter your state of consciousness via entheogens and other intoxicants. Marijuana works well with mantras, for instance.

In Buddhist areas of the Himalayas, you can often find mani stones, stones inscribed with mantras and left as offerings to spirits of place or to provide protection. Sigils can be used in a similar fashion. Several times I have used my trusty gold paint pen with stones collected on the holy isle of Anglesey and left these along the Thames near my house. Mytho-poetically, Thames comes from *Thamesis* or "Isis" which is actually why I adapted the above aretalogy in the first place; she is the patron goddess of London's great river. Be considerate going down the mani stone route. *Genius loci* have their own agendas and existences to lead. They may react ambivalently to you leaving your enchantments around.

One of the more common questions I am asked is what to do if you only have one or two sigils you wish to activate. Here is where you can indulge in some of the flippancy that gives chaos magic such a bad name. There are always pointless things to enchant for: spotting celebrities when you are out on the town, getting a seat on the tube or bus, freebies in restaurants. If these ideas do not take your fancy, then try for something a little more lofty. Consider sigilising holy or empowering phrases such as "every man and every woman is a star." Even song lyrics will do at a pinch. It is your head after all.

HOW TO WAGE
A MIND WAR

"I came here to chew bubblegum and kick ass.
And I'm all out of bubblegum."

JOHN NADA, *THEY LIVE*

Management theory, as we have come to know it and be subject to it, began on the slave plantations in the Caribbean and southern states. According to Harvard Business School researcher Caitlin Rosenthal, it was the request for regular reports by the absentee landlords of Jamaican and Barbadan plantations that led to the modern separation of *management* and *ownership* ... one of the hallmarks of modern capitalism.[62] It was in

---

62   Caitlin Rosenthal. "Plantations Practiced Modern Management." *Harvard Business Review*. September 2013.

this milieu that managers first kept details records of a human's *worth* and *cost*. A strapping young man may pick more cotton but also eats more than a couple of cheaper, older women. Which purchase was the most cost effective over time? Slave owners could collect data on their workforces that no one else could because the "employees" were locked in from cradle to grave. Northern workers subject to such extreme monitoring would have simply quit. The increase in data led slave owners to experiment with output optimisation techniques like small cash prizes for whichever slave picked the most cotton—call it the "slave of the month" programme—that are still in use today.

This ghoulish origin story is one of the many reasons I reject the word "hack." Business hacks, like so-called life hacks, inevitably boil down to silly little habits designed to fit more *work* into your day. They are descendants of a highly dubious family line and contribute nothing of true value to your life. There is a reason there is no such thing as a "meaning hack" and it is because you cannot short-circuit the quest for life's meaning by learning a few new tips to optimise your inbox. Four-hour work weeks, keeping your cubicle clean, wearing a tie on Fridays... these are all demonic devices that trick you into thinking the illusion of control is the same thing as life meaning.

In the same boat as these appalling hacks we can place any of those single Big Idea books that became popular about a decade ago—ones to do with being fooled by uncertainty that are, at best, inflated versions of feature articles from Sunday papers. Either they are based on rapidly dismissed scientific "evidence" or they are published by out-and-out liars. Jonah Lehrer was proved to be plagiarising. Malcolm Gladwell's name appears on an early 90s third-party message development list for tobacco lobbyists, i.e., a list of journalists who can be relied upon to create sympathetic content. This is around the time he was writing pro-tobacco industry pieces in the *Washington Post*. Imagine that. Any of these so-called business success books appear to only provide advice in how to be successful shilling business books. You have to go back almost a century before you find popular finance advice that isn't worse than useless.

As for the Internet's consensus on how to achieve financial success in a knowledge economy or creative economy or whatever word we use to describe an economy with a hollowed-out manufacturing base, this appears to only have relevance to college-educated white boys looking to found a startup described as "Uber for scooters" while their girlfriends financially support them by working at social media agencies.

What is so astounding about this entire industry is that it is selling you unachievable ways to get a life you do not even want in the first place. Seriously, let's look at the life you are supposed to have.

A Recommended Life

Everyone wants a unique life. They want outcomes that are different from the norm: wealth, health, longevity. And yet the approach to getting outcomes different from the norm appears to be by approaching life in the same way everyone else does. This is bad strategy and bad magic. Here are the phases of a recommended existence.

1. Apply yourself diligently in a schooling system built to turn out factory workers in the nineteenth century that now cannot even do that.

2. Earn a college degree that guarantees "good, safe employment."

3. Have a "career" working your way up through large, stable corporations.

4. Use your below-inflation-growth salary to acquire a mortgage for a suburban home from which you commute to your "career" using high amounts of increasingly expensive energy.

5. Fill your mortgaged house with appliances and offspring so that the cycle may perpetuate.

6. Allow inflation to convince you that your suburban house has appreciated in value so that you can sell it and move either to a larger one if you still have offspring or a smaller one if you don't.

7. See Europe on a coach tour with other Americans at some stage.

8. Die.

Right away you can see some problems. Firstly, the life on offer is awful! Secondly, the parts of the plan that rely on society's promise to you have long since gone. The education system is a mess, the college system is the very definition of extortion, stable white-collar employment no longer exists, energy is prohibitively expensive, and housing is not an investment but *at best* an inflation hedge.

Why then does it melt everyone's faces if you *dare* to suggest that there might be another way to achieve a life different to this one? The answer inevitably comes down to one of those trendy Big Ideas you could write a bestselling life hack book about—herd bias, especially if you use evolutionary psychology to tie it back to our evolution out of monkey troops.

Herd bias is an unbecoming trait in a magician. One does not meet the devil at the crossroads to build a life that looks like everyone else's. Too often people confuse their current circumstances for their fate. To be sure, our current circumstances are not all that rosy but that just gives us our starting position. Here is where magic departs from the religious beliefs—such as Paganism—that frequently house it; it has an unavoidable moral ambiguity to practical enchantment that I am anything but ambiguous about. Your current lack of success *might* be the will of the gods, but you are still going to do everything in your power to change it. I often think about our magical ancestors and the social and economic upheavals they had to go through. Consider what life was like for the wandering sorcerer during the collapse of the Roman empire or the Pembrokeshire cunning man during the industrial revolution and let them be your inspiration. Yes, the world is changing—possibly even *collapsing*. We would all prefer a better economic environment in which to thrive, but this is the one we have. It does not change the game, only the plays.

As for what this chapter is doing in a book about magic, let me give you some medical advice. Never ask your doctor what he or she thinks you should do. Ask them what *they* would do in your situation. The suggestions below are what I would do in your situation because I am in your situation and this is what I have done. Magic, like the cosmic equivalent of medical lubricant it really is, has been liberally applied at every probabilistic friction point in my work life. And it has turned out quite all right, to be honest. Adam Braun, whose nonprofit built 150 schools in developing countries before his thirty-first birthday, says "big dreams start with small, unreasonable acts."[63]

For any of these unreasonable acts to appear palatable, something needs to break in the magician's mind. It typically happens sometime after having that first inciting incident or initiation. There arises the permanent realisation that the promise of the world is not only bullshit but is also empty. To not act on this realisation, to not deploy what you have learned about the malleability of the manifest universe, is to be a mechanic without a car. What's the point?

A defining characteristic of the most prominent magicians of fiction and reality is that they meddle. Dee, Crowley, Merlin, Gandalf, Morgan Le Fay, Bruno. Whatever the weather, they went out to remake the universe in a way that suited them better. We must do the same. Whatever the macroeconomic conditions, the magician must always heed the advice of *Firefly*'s Captain Mal Reynolds: aim to misbehave.

---

63   Adam Braun. *The Promise of a Pencil: How an Ordinary Person Can Create Extraordinary Change.* Scribner, 2014.

Be Brave, Not Reckless

Whilst writing this book, I met an American corporate lawyer in a castle in France and attempted to explain to her what I was writing about. She told me she would never buy it for her nieces because it sounded too grim. In her mind, nothing good could come of telling her nieces the truth of the economic reality they would face as they entered adulthood. Fine. Frankly, I don't think it sounds grim enough. I don't think it is grim enough because it offers a huge advantage: knowledge. Your advantage is knowledge, and no one can take that from you.

Knowledge in this case is a confident understanding of the probabilistic nature of the universe, a reasonable understanding of your current probabilities of successful outcomes and the capacity to unblinkingly act on the calculated risks that flow from both these understandings.

I say "calculated risk" but actually you cannot calculate risk, not really. What you can instead calculate is fragility. An object or person can be defined as fragile if it responds negatively to volatility. Nassim Nicholas Taleb uses the famous example of the teacup.[64] Teacups do not like volatility. For the fragile, shocks bring higher and higher harm. Nothing happens to a teacup most of the time, but when it does happen, it is overwhelmingly negative: it breaks. (The impact of volatility also rarely shows up in the history of the product: you can't tell that a teacup will smash by looking at its behaviour before it does. Similarly, volatile events like redundancies rarely show up in the history of you.) The goal of the magician, particularly the chaos magician, is to position his or her life so that it responds positively to volatility rather than negatively. Volatility should make your life better, not worse, just as the thousands of microtears in your muscles during weight training lead to larger biceps. Be the bicep, not the teacup! It's easier than it sounds, and it gets easier the further you stray from society's recommended life.

---

64   Nassim Nicholas Taleb. *Antifragile: Things That Gain From Disorder*. Penguin, 2013.

As for those who do not consider themselves risk takers, this reflects a fundamental misunderstanding of both risk and their own personalities. The appetite for risk exists on a spectrum, it is not binary. You may be so comfortable taking certain risks that you do not consider them risks at all, like smokers at the airport worrying about their flight, or patrons expressing concern over terrorism in the pub before driving home drunk. The other side of this inability to see risks you are comfortable with as inherently risky is the propensity to see risks that make you uncomfortable as much riskier than they are.

Consider the following. You may think these strategies are a bit too extreme, a bit too *risky*, and decide that getting massively into debt to buy an inflation hedge you can live in on the outskirts of your home town is "more you." You don't want to be doing anything with all these risky strategies. The thing about how economies work is that not taking a position is still taking a position. By refusing to adjust your strategy from the recommended life offered to the baby boomers forty years ago, what you are saying is that you have every confidence in the system; the current challenges are just temporary, and someone will come and sort it all out for us. That strikes me as extremely risky, riskier than putting it all on black. Is toeing the line being brave or is it being reckless? You cannot duck risk. There are no civilians in a mind war.

Here is the difference between bravery and recklessness. If you are not taking risks, you are failing to find the opportunities you are looking for, you are denying yourself *optionality*. In a career setting, this looks like taking on side projects at night and on weekends, being visible at industry events, putting your hand up for international assignments, applying for jobs you think you are under-qualified for, or even just asking the boss for extra work that stretches you.

Bravery, when combined with alertness, manifests in the highly desirable state of being "lucky." It is not just the chance meeting with a potential employer at a friend's birthday party, it is following through on that initial contact. It is replying to a blog commenter who had an observation about some industry news you had posted. The executive director of the Stanford Technology Ventures Program, Tina Seelig, observes that being lucky is actually a way of being in the world.[65] It is also one that you can cultivate through the combination of risk-taking and observation. "Lucky" people are more willing to try things outside their usual experience which—and it sounds obvious when it is written down—is how they end up with atypical life outcomes like greater wealth and happiness. Stay open to the unexpected, be ready to pounce on unusual opportunities and always keep a bottle of abre camino oil to hand.

To be brave implies taking actions that have inherent risk, that may not go your way. This is as it should be. Recall that another name for capitalism might as well be "riskism." The economic system is—or at least was—designed to reward capital that is placed at risk through investment. The problem is most people confuse risk with "too much risk," especially when it comes to achieving their so-called dreams. People confuse taking a risk with risking it all. Particularly for those with creative aspirations, doing only what you love is terrible advice as it exposes you to much, much more downside from risk than there is upside. Achieving financial success through creativity is a very low-probability outcome that in many cases is ultimately self-defeating as it becomes increasingly difficult to sculpt or write a novel when you are worried about being homeless at the end of the week.

Instead, consider the following. Trial and error is the intelligence of chaos. If you wish to increase your optionality, if you wish to build "lucky" behaviours, then you are going to need to be placing multiple bets on multiple successful outcomes. You cannot do this for very long if each of the bets are too large. Invest in multiple bets that expose you to only a small

65   Jocelyn K. Glei. *Maximize Your Potential: Grow Your Expertise, Take Bold Risks &*
      Build an Incredible Career. Lake Union Publishing, 2013.

amount of downside and a greater possibility of upside than one large bet. Do not quit your job to found a design agency, volunteer your design skills one evening a week for three separate charities or nonprofits.

Trial and error is the intelligence of chaos because your mistakes are *information*. The more of them you make, the more information you have to make the next round. Aim for as many mistakes as possible that cost you the least amount possible. Almost any situation you find yourself in can be improved and even turned around with a combination of persistence and increased information.

Optionality is applying the intelligence of chaos. As Taleb observes, you do not actually need to know precisely where you are going if you have upside, if an unexpected event *benefits* you more than it *harms* you. This is a hugely beneficial way of living in a probabilistic universe if you experiment where the losses can be minimised and the gains are very large. Returning to my persistent heresy against the one true religion of property ownership, an excellent example is the real estate landscape in London or New York. The salaries on offer are orders of magnitude greater than anywhere else in their respective countries, but the multiple of those salaries for the average property price is higher still. Moving to a high income economy enables you to shoot for much more individual wealth than in a smaller economic area. You minimise the risk associated with high salary/high risk careers by renting. Yes, rents are extremely high, but you still have not surrendered your personal optionality in being able to reduce rental overhead or even leave the city if you lose your high salary position. (You can also take higher salary positions elsewhere in the world more easily than someone struggling with property debt.) Over twenty years, exposure to an economy with extremely high salaries makes rent the investment everyone seems to think it isn't.

If you want to be rich, move to where people get rich and then do not get into debt. If you want something different for your life, the same unemotional examination is required.

Housing

We have already covered why the mortgage industry exists and it is not for our benefit. We have also shown that as an investment it performs very poorly, offering you an inflation hedge at best. This is more about where and how to physically live—an unavoidable subject for all but the most ardent modern nomads. So that I am not misunderstood, property *ownership* is an effective store of value over the long term. Acquiring very high amounts of debt in an economy undergoing permanent, structural changes is too risky and too limiting. This is the great taboo of individual wealth. Here is what author and entrepreneur James Altucher has to say about it on his blog:

> *Buying coffee on the street instead of in a Starbucks is the poor man's way to get rich. In other words, you will never get rich by scratching out ten cents from your dollar. People save 10 cents on a coffee and then ....overpay $100,000 for a house and then do reconstruction on it. Or they save 10 cents on a book and then ... buy a college degree that they never use for $200,000.*[66]

Having somewhere to live is obviously essential to living your preferred life and in markets where the customer *has* to participate—health, housing, food, and the like—dangers, cartels, and complexities rule. So let us consider the following thought exercise, based on a scenario outlined on Charles Hugh-Smith's popular economics blog, *Of Two Minds:*.

> *A family with a household income of $80,000 sits just in the top 30% of all households. If this household bought at the top of the market, it has a huge mortgage, credit cards, auto loans for two cars. Servicing this debt in addition to combined utilities leaves very little for dining out or going on vacation, especially if the parents are contributing*

---

66   James Altucher. "The Secrets of Personal Finance. "Accessed April 12, 2015. www.jamesaltucher.com/2014/09/the-secrets-of-personal-finance/

*to college education for their kids. Measured in terms of the items
this family (currently) legally owns they appear wealthy. However
subtracting their debt obligations paints a picture of a family on the
breadline that spends much of their incarnation servicing debt with
little money to actually live their lives over the forty years of debt
servicing. This is a family that is one negative health diagnosis or
even minor auto accident away from disaster. This family is a teacup.*

An alternative is not only possible, can we even call it an alternative
in the world that has emerged around us? Try these.

*Americans buy too much house. The average home size has
increased by 50% in the last two decades, mostly in an effort to get
people to take out larger and larger mortgages. They are now more
than three times the size of the average house in the UK. You do not
need this much house! You also need to be aware of how much of
your future wealth will be absorbed by property taxes on a house
that is either unnecessarily large or in an over-valued area. That is
wealth that could go to making art or magic or having adventures.*

Consider instead multi-generational or multi-family ownership. For
all but the last sixty years, the entire history of human habitation has been
multi-generational. The notion that a "real" American families lives on its
own in a large house in the suburbs is a fifty-year-old Madison Avenue
creation for a singular national market. The Danish, for instance, have been
doing cohousing for more than half a century. Multi-occupancy or multi-
ownership arrangement provide additional redundancy if one person loses
their income or has a poor health diagnosis. Multi-ownership should ideally shorten the mortgage period down to three to five years, beyond which
you begin to skew your risk. It also provides additional flexibility should
one or more person need to move temporarily for work. Additionally, it
kickstarts a return to intergenerational capital pooling, which has been

the secret of wealthy families' success since the rise of cities more than five thousand years ago. Return to Charles Hugh-Smith:

> *The solution to the erosion of the middle class lifestyle is to destroy debt and other fixed costs and eliminate self-sabotaging discretionary consumption that cripples the household's ability to accumulate capital that generates income. There is nothing magical about the values and behaviors that enable this; it boils down to choosing to leave the permanent adolescence of debt-based consumerism behind and move up to a more prosperous, productive way of living: doing more with less.*[67]

Thirty-five percent of Americans have debt in collection. Three-quarters live paycheck to paycheck. Almost half cannot cover a $400 expense without going into debt or selling something.[68] You really have to ask yourself whether living in such a precarious situation is weirder than buying a house with your brother and his wife.

On a related note, it is regularly reported that one in four college graduates still live with their parents in the years after college. What is unclear to me is how this is a bad thing for anyone but landlords and mortgage sellers. Since we started living in huts we have been living in multi-generational dwellings. Are young people expected to do the opposite just as they face increased economic headwinds? (I left home when I was eighteen, by the way. And have moved countries several times since then. Lest you think this is an exercise in self-justification.)

The second essential transformation of the domestic space comes with the rise of edible landscapes. Nothing would make me happier than driving

---

67   Charles Hugh-Smith. "The Solution to the Declining Middle Class: Destroy Fixed Costs and Debt." Accessed April 12, 2015. charleshughsmith.blogspot .co.uk/2014/05/the-solution-to-declining-middle-class.html.

68   Michael Snyder. "Job = Just Over Broke." Accessed April 17, 2015. www .zerohedge.com/news/2014-08-13/job-just-over-broke.

through the suburbs and seeing the lawns and hedges replaced with out-of-control pumpkin and cucumber vines. An unavoidable reality of life in the early twenty-first century is that the cost of food is increasing even as its quality in decreasing. Collectively, we need to get over the white people cringe that growing one's own food is "something immigrants do." Here is another activity which is almost entirely upside. Learn about, grow, and eat your own food. No space is too small.

Education

After the housing crash of 2008, the banksters were in need of a new source of debt to impose on Americans and then securitize into financial instruments of mass destruction. They found it. College debt exceeds that of all credit card debt and auto loans in the US. It is also the only form of debt that follows you after bankruptcy. This debt is now being securitised, just as subprime mortgages were, because it remains the only sufficient quantity of debt the general population appears willing to accrue.

The whole situation is ghastly. Tuition fees have risen 300 percent versus the (already manipulated) Consumer Price Index between 1990 and 2011. Thirty-seven percent of students fail to finish with a degree, meaning they are burdened with unavoidable debt for a product they never actually received.[69] As states push through more funding cuts, universities raise their rates for a product that is getting less and less useful.

Even the Federal Reserve itself is suggesting a college degree is not be the universal panacea everyone once considered it to be. In May 2014, the Federal Reserve Bank of San Francisco noted that incomes for the bottom 25 percent of all bachelor's graduates do not outperform the incomes of those without a college degree and given the additional debt burden the

---

69   Karen L. Cates. "Let's Start Telling Young People the Truth about College." Accessed April 17, 2015. www.bloomberg.com/bw/articles/2014-07-16/stop -feeding-high-school-students-the-myth-that-college-is-right-for-everyone.

graduates have, college becomes a poor financial perspective for this segment.[70] They go on to suggest that the numbers do not hold for the incomes of the remaining graduates, but this is a misunderstanding of mathematics that can only come from a central banker.

In fact, once the costs of attending college are considered, it is likely that earning a bachelor's degree would not have been a good investment for many in the lowest 25 percent of college graduate wage earners. Of course, what goes unsaid is that these numbers repeat until you only end up with one student left in the whole country. If the bottom 25 percent *didn't* go to college, then the bottom quarter of the remaining 75 percent would be in the same situation when it comes to average wages which would have now risen for those who didn't go to college.

In any other category of business, to have such high costs and such an astoundingly poor success rate would quickly lead to mass closures. Instead the higher education industry insists it is cost-effective and helpful for students even as all evidence points to the contrary. As Charles Hugh-Smith notes, tertiary education functions in an identical fashion to any other cartel: colleges maintain a monopoly on accreditation.[71] There is no accountability for a poor product because you cannot buy it anywhere else.

And it is a product. A university can only issue a credential that is seen as a proxy for knowledge. Its relationship to any underlying knowledge is tenuous and its stamp of authenticity is largely redundant in a post-LinkedIn world. Google, for instance, no longer asks job applicants for GPAs or academic transcripts because they do not predict anything. There is no measurable correlation between success in college exams and success later in life. When it comes to successful people who have been through the college

---

70 Tyler Durden, (pseud). "Federal Reserve Warns That 'College May Not Pay Off For Everyone.'" Accessed April 17, 2015. www.zerohedge.com/news/2014-09-04 /federal-reserve-warns-college-may-not-pay-everyone.

71 Charles Hugh-Smith. *Get a Job, Build a Career and Defy a Bewildering Economy.* Createspace Independent Publishing Platform, 2014.

system, Taleb refers to this as "teaching birds how to fly."[72] Imagine a business professor standing up in front of an auditorium, teaching a room full of birds about flight. At the end of his lecture he flings open the doors and all his students fly out. He thinks he has taught them about flying, but they were already birds.

If you are from a very wealthy family then, by all means, go to an elite college and milk it for network effects. Given that you are reading this particular book, it is unlikely that is the case, so think about the following. What we have with the tertiary education sector is a misunderstanding of scarcity. College degrees used to be scarce when in-person tuition and the oral transmission of knowledge was required. There were fewer people with degrees than there were jobs that required them. Today the opposite is true. Fewer jobs, more degrees than needed. This leads to degree inflation, which compounds the student debt burden and makes the entire system appear *more* essential. Where once a job required only a high school education, now it requires a bachelor's degree. Jobs previously requiring a bachelor's degree now insist on a master's degree, and so on. Thus the cartel that caused the problem also appears as its seeming solution. Your vast amount of student debt didn't get you the job you want? Then come back and have some *more* debt! Nice work if you can get it.

What's scarce today is real-world experience or even, it turns out, real-world *preparedness*. The number of students exiting the college system with poor literacy skills is amazing, to say nothing of those entering it. Should you wish to pursue interests that require specific degrees, then a strategy that is equally radical to the above housing suggestion is required.

- If you are not from a rich family, then do not do the next best thing. Do the *opposite* thing. Make your college experience as cheap as possible. An online degree is fine if it is just a bullet point on a résumé otherwise filled with

---

72   Nassim Nicholas Taleb. *Antifragile: Things That Gain From Disorder*. Penguin, 2013.

successful projects and proof of capability. People will tell you education is getting expensive. Education has never been cheaper or more readily available in human history; a college *degree* has never been more expensive.

- Be employed or minimise your debt as much as possible. Graduating with too much debt severely affects your optionality.

- If you are paying all that money, you should use the experience as an excuse to launch a bunch of projects. Upon graduation, you must be able to prove your experience. Is the dry cleaner still using the logo you designed? Is the soup kitchen still using the logistics plan you built for them?

- Internships, properly used, deserve their own bullet point. Much ink has been spilled decrying them as zero-cost labour and white privilege. They are probably both of those things. They are also advantageous if used correctly. In fact, according to a large-scale résumé study by University of Wisconsin economist John M. Nunley, having a business degree listed on a résumé did not improve the chances of getting a call for an interview at all but listing interning experience improved the chances by 14 percent.[73] If you can meet the devil at the crossroads, you can choke down your dignity for a spot of interning.

73   John M. Nunley et al. "College Major, Internship Experience, and Employment Opportunities: Estimates from a Résumé Audit." *Auburn University Department of Economics Working Paper Series.* Accessed April 17, 2015. cla.auburn.edu /econwp/archives/2014/2014-03.pdf.

- Use your time at college to network. Wealthy families come with built-in networks. The rest of us have to build them ourselves. If you are a wallflower, too bad. Get better at it. That is what alcohol is for.

Now that I have gotten that off the chest, let us talk about *learning* rather than simply college. Given that I did a film degree that did not even have exams on the other side of the world from where I currently live, let me say that I regret almost every minute of it. The few minutes I do not regret are when I interned at Fox Studios and learned how to do audio post-production by listening to Christopher Lloyd say the same half a line over and over again until I found the correct one. (It had been mislabelled during production.) Or it was when I shot a documentary about a sunken city and had to work out how to convince two separate kings and one government minister to allow me access to the sites.

Projects and continual learning are the stakes plunged into the ground that demarcate your area of expertise. I have not been asked about my university experience in almost fifteen years. In the meantime I have presented global media and content strategy all over Europe and been acquired by a publicly listed American media company. My degree probably taught me nothing. My experience on the documentary helps me every day.

This book emerged from the success—such as it is—of my blog. And the blog emerged from being made redundant from Discovery Channel. I figured it would be good to improve my understanding of web publishing and I had some time on my hands. Should I do a course or should I just *do it?* Continual learning is not the process of accruing a growing pile of certificates in project management and MS Office proficiency and so on—although they can help. Continual learning arises when you refuse to let circumstances or other people's opinions of you stand in your way. Like being lucky, it lives entirely in a singular mindset: do not worry about being good at something. Focus instead on getting better at it. The rest is upside.

Exposure to the New Economy

When Chinese ecommerce platform Alibaba submitted its IPO paperwork in advance of its 2014 stock market listing, it had 231 million active buyers, a volume of buyers greater than the adult population of the United States. More than two billion people have access to the web via mobile devices, and the total number of users is greater in developing countries than it is in developed ones. In all of human history there has never been so large a market of potential customers and business partners.

All of this is to say that you simultaneously live in more than one economy. Historically we have measured economies exclusively based on place—there is a recession in New Zealand, youth unemployment is declining in Paris—because all economies were based around place almost by definition. Today, multiple economies overlay the same geographic area. There is the economy of travel agents and newspaper printers that is dying and there is the rapidly growing, multi-trillion dollar economy that is fast emerging. It falls to you to decide which one you would prefer greater exposure to. Forget the unemployment figures you see on the news. According to the CEO of Gallup, the number of US adults employed for more than thirty hours a week is only 42 percent. "Official" unemployment data will suggest only around 8 percent unemployment. But there are 93 million considered not in the labor force. A report prepared by Global Insight for the 2014 United States Conference of Mayors shows that the new jobs being added pay 23 percent less than the jobs being lost at a national level.[74]

You are being intellectually dishonest with yourself if you think that pockets of hyper-growth occurring in places beyond where you currently live are irrelevant. They are not. A very obvious opportunity is staring you in the face. Move.

---

74   Global Insights. "US Metro Economies: Income and Wage Gaps Across the US." August 2014. www.usmayors.org/metroeconomies/2014/08/report.pdf.

It is surprising that this option does not occur to people more often. During our lifetime—in fact in the last few years—we have experienced one of the biggest demographic changes in the human journey: for the first time ever we are now a majority urban species. Economic migration is the reality of the human condition. Opportunity is not evenly distributed and if you happen to live somewhere where there is less of it then you need to move. As with all economics, not taking a position is still taking a position. Refusing to move is taking the position that you will make do with the reduced or entirely absent opportunities in the area where you currently live.

One of the benefits of living in an age of Big Data is that much of the intellectual heavy lifting surrounding moving has been done for you. An evening spent with a bottle of wine and a search engine will result in an opportunity grid of potential new locations. Often these locations are counter-intuitive. Yes, New York will see the highest growth in low-wage service roles but parts of Florida, Washington, and Texas metro areas offer the highest potential for middle class job growth in the next decade. Raleigh, North Carolina, has been identified as an emerging tech hub (along with Eindhoven in the Netherlands if you are looking further afield). Atlanta basically already is one.

There have been periods in our recent history where our ancestors did things like walk across the Dust Bowl to find work as grave diggers. Today, in an age of affordable air travel and high speed Internet access, the propensity to move for employment is actually *declining*. Only 20 percent of today's 25–34-year-olds moved for work, down from 31 percent in 1965.[75] In a 2014 interview with Bloomberg, Carsey Institute demographer Kenneth Johnson said, "Migration is a key advantage of the American system historically. The ability of growing areas to attract migrants from a large

---

75 Steve Matthews and Victoria Stilwell. "America on the Move Becomes Stay-
Home Nation for Young: Economy." Accessed April 17, 2015. www.bloomberg
.com/news/articles/2014-05-12/america-on-the-move-becomes-stay-at-home
-nation-for-millennials.

national labor pool has historically helped the US adapt to changing economic conditions."[76]

A common pushback to the idea of moving for work is that it is disruptive to one's children. Maybe so, but the life outcomes are significantly worse for children who were raised in poverty versus children who moved several times during their schooling. If that is your only excuse, it is flimsy. Think very carefully on the possibility that you are using children's natural resistance to change as a cover for your own unwillingness.

Between 1990 and 2013, disposable income rose 0 percent and rent rose 15 percent.[77] A willingness to move offers you additional valves to reduce your cost of living pressure. It also becomes clearer how the mind war strategies work in concert: move to a high growth area with close friends or family, rent and live together, diversify your incomes, share costs, stay out of debt. A world in which opportunity is not randomly distributed that also has a working age population displaying less interest in chasing after it presents a significant strategic advantage for the ambitious magician. Resist the atomizing effect of monoculture's celebration of the fiction of the individual. This is how tribes work, this is how it has always been done. Nomadism is humanity's natural state and adventurism is wizardry's natural one.

Seek Convexity

Convex work is simply the sort of work that has the highest revenue upswing potential from the initial investment. If you open a dive bar in Saudi Arabia you will be confronted with an immediate and fairly low revenue ceiling. If you open one in Hoxton, London, you will not. The same goes with personal or vocational investment. Given the demographic changes facing the western world in the next twenty years, is it better to specialise

---

76 Matthews and Stilwell, ibid.

77 Tyler Durden (pseud). "Where Disposable Income Goes to Die: Since 1990 Real Rents Are Up 15% While Median Incomes Are Unchanged." Accessed April 17, 2015. www.zerohedge.com/news/2014-07-02/where-disposable-income-goes-die-1990-real-rents-are-15-while-median-incomes-are-unc.

in gerontological nursing or adolescent nursing? For the *same* initial investment, which option has even the tiniest chance of you owning a network of old folks homes and retiring to a private island?

A caveat to seeking vocational convexity relating also to choosing where to live is to be aware of whether there is an oversupply in the medium term. In challenging economic times, masses of people retrain...typically in "sounds good on paper" pointlessnesses like MBAs or law degrees. Because the world needs more of them, eh? Just be aware that the oversupply may hit the job market before you can even get there.

Next, robot-proof yourself. This cannot be over-emphasised. Your new hobby needs to be keeping up with robotics news. The only type of work that cannot currently be robotised is that which has an unknown point of completion. An operation where a dental filling is replaced has a known point of completion: a new filling. A new summer menu or a garden design does not. In the next decade, robotics will affect the middle income workforce a lot more than you currently think *but* slightly less than you currently fear. For the open-eyed, there is opportunity here: when asked how he would prepare for a match against a computer, Dutch chess master Jan Hein Donner said, "I would bring a hammer."[78] Jan will probably still have a job in ten years time.

Mercifully, seeking convexity does away with the preposterous and dangerous fiction that you must only do work that you are passionate about, that you must follow this passion at all costs. If this were in any way a solution we would not have teenagers and kids in their early twenties dropping out of college—as the majority of them do—with incomplete degrees and massive debt burdens. The assumption that a child has a pre-existing passion is as flawed as the assumption that such passions align with ways of making money either today or in the near future. On an individual level,

---

78   Erik Brynjolfsson and Andrew Mcafee. *The Second Machine Age: Work, Progress, and Prosperity in a Time of Brilliant Technologies.* W. W. Norton & Company, 2014.

seeking convexity means "developing rare and valuable skills." Scarcity always carries a premium. If you have in-demand skills then you can leverage them to engineer either the type of career or the type of life you wish to lead. Not everyone considers the largest possible salary as their primary goal. My accountant does not work Fridays because he likes to surf. I cannot do what he does, so I don't get accounting services on Fridays. "Developing rare and valuable skills" lacks some of the romance of finding your destiny in a lifetime role that brings you happiness and wealth, but it has the strategic advantage of actually working. Especially when you combine it with the mind war strategy of taking charge of your own training and experience. Just as with housing and where you locate yourself, mind wars are invariably fought on multiple fronts.

From Convexity to Mastery

A common and highly suspect objection to the strategy of cultivating industry non-specific "rare and valuable skills" is that it smacks of dilettantism. Hardly. You have only a finite number of years in the workforce (and in your life!) so you must be highly intolerant of stagnation. If a project or a business or a job does not turn out the way you want or need it to, abandon it. In creative writing this is "killing your darlings." In business this is good business. One of business writer Seth Godin's best yet least-understood books, *The Dip*, describes how you should abandon anything you are not going to be best in the world at as soon as you realise this is so. Hyperbole, perhaps, but still a very good way of assessing which skills and projects you choose to focus your time on. Thus is mastery achieved with enough time to put it to use engineering the life you wish to lead.

In the Workplace

More or less every piece of workplace advice you have been given is either wrong or suited to more predictable economic times. Workplace advice is really human behavioural advice: how to regulate your own and how to shape that of others. Given that early twenty-first century workplaces run the full gamut from Alaskan crab fishing fleets to the International Space Station, there are a surprisingly high number of universal approaches worth incorporating into your mind war. Here are some personal observations from reasonably successful campaigns across multiple industries in five separate countries (so far).

- **Personal finances.** You are sunk before you begin without a working knowledge of your own finances and tax laws. I know it is boring. Too bad.

- **Project management.** Everything is a project. Your whole incarnation is a project. There is an abundance of free project management resources and training available on the Internet. Consider investing in certification as it only costs a few hundred dollars. There isn't a workplace on earth that could not benefit from a better understanding of project management among its employees.

- **Opportunity cost.** Learn what it is and always be calculating it. Especially in the occult world, there are too many micro-businesses that allegedly break even but consume huge amounts of time and energy that could be better allocated elsewhere ... thus freeing up more time for the hobbies people are so desperate to turn into businesses so they can spend more time on them.

- **Actively seek problems to solve.** Complete or solve problems either in your workplace or for real-world groups if your current job status does not allow for independent problem solving (though I would struggle to find examples of such workplaces even in low skill industries). Do not show up and expect to be told what to do—that is what robots are for.

- **Job titles are a trap.** Experience is more important. Engineering your résumé to reflect a progression of job titles you think are in demand is a hugely risky strategy, as the job you are aiming for may not exist in two years' time. Focus instead on what you want to accomplish. "Launching an m-commerce store in Brazil" is vastly more impressive than "Mobile Product Manager: LatAm." In every role, ask yourself, "What problem am I solving?"

- **If your job does not offer scope for additional responsibilities, volunteer at a church or food bank.** The days of juniors being "groomed" for senior positions are long over. It is questionable whether they existed at all beyond the limited sphere of nepotism in family-owned businesses. No one is going to spend more time thinking about or caring for your career than you. No one.

- **Be healthy.** This means more than "do not be fat," but it also means that too. People who are overweight are paid less than those who aren't. I dislike this as much as the next guy who has struggled with his weight his whole life, but the numbers do not lie. As for a wider definition of health, the evidence that regular physical activity improves mental and emotional performance is overwhelming. Spending time at the gym is the same thing as putting in extra hours at the office. Additionally, Americans make up only 5 percent of the planet's population but consume more than half of all pharmaceuticals. This rises to 80 percent when it comes to prescription painkillers. Be healthy so you do not need to be stoned at work. That alone will leapfrog you over most of the competition.

- **Learn to compartmentalise.** The reason business is called business rather than "fun" is that sometimes it isn't. Especially with the looming demographic and economic changes the economy is undergoing, you will need to be very good at compartmentalisation. A chaos magic approach to multiple selves is particularly useful in separating your work from your non-work life. Be warned. It gets murky out there.

- **General roles are preferable to specialist ones when it comes to promotion.** Getting caught in "functional silos" like legal or comms or human resources is more likely to cap your promotional opportunities. Get a wide variety of operational experience and ensure you have P & L responsibility.

- **Gain international experience.** Most top executives have international experience. Plus it's fun.

- **Marry well.** This does not mean marry above your station, it means find a spouse/partner who can function as a solid support system at home. Top executives may not always have children, but they almost always have a supportive spouse.

- **Avoid the workplace pariah.** You will recognise the workplace pariah as the one who befriends you the second you join a business. Just like in a game of poker, if you don't know who the workplace pariah is … guess what?

- **Never complain about your boss.** Ever. Similarly, be above office politics. If you want to complain about people, get a therapist.

- **Be aware of your class indicators.** People promote those who are similar to themselves. Table manners, which television programmes you watch, where you holiday, which sports you play, these are hugely important. Not too many senior executives eat pizza at their desk while talking with their mouth full about the NASCAR-themed cruise they took last year. Americans have an unfortunate tendency to confuse class with wealth. Wealth is not required for the most important class indicators.

- **Have a game plan, but keep it secret.** It has never been clear to me why some people think vocalising how ambitious they are will assist them with their ambition. It won't. See above about class indicators.

The Network

People who do not understand networking think it is handing out business cards at conferences or retweeting industry opinion makers. Networks are not measured in the volume of people that you have met. Networks are an accumulation of social capital. For instance, the true value of elite education is located in the advantage of matriculating—and drinking and committing sexual assault in fraternity basements—with the scions of hyper-connected, wealthy families. Thus are future presidents selected.

It is a mistake to think that you are hired by a company. In actuality, you are hired by a person. All opportunity flows through people. The underlying spirit of the network is generosity, not reciprocity. An unthinking approach to network is to assume a tit-for-tat response to somebody doing you a favour. The ROI of your network is far less predictable. Help people with no expectation of reward because, as Executive Director of Harvard's Saguaro Seminar, Thomas Sanders, notes: the underlying network science suggests that it is the weak links rather than the strong ones who deliver the best return.[79] It is the friend of the friend of the friend who happens to have

---

79   Thomas Sanders. "Why weak ties are strong for job searches." Accessed April 17, 2015. socialcapital.wordpress.com/2011/09/27/why-weak-ties-are-strong-for -job-searches.

your perfect job opportunity. You will never know in advance which permutation of weak links will deliver this. Trying to keep some kind of Santa Claus-style grudge list is a waste of time. This is how global networking expert Sunny Bates explains it:

> *It's very easy to think that somebody knows you. And that if they know you, they will think about calling you, or asking you, or wanting you for something. But people forget. I was a headhunter for many years, and I was always amazed because easily 20 percent of the time, the final person who was hired was well-known to the client. (They just hadn't thought about them.) That means that, for every five people you know, one is likely to have an impact on you or hire you—that should make you want to expand your circle.*[80]

In a mind war, networking extends far beyond having more than 500 LinkedIn connections. Correctly used, it is probably one of our greatest advantages. From a magical perspective, I have my professional network, but I consider it a subset of something larger and more varied. I consider it part of my tribe. It is too early to predict just how disruptive the rise of crowdfunding and the return of localism is going to be, but they are hugely positive signals that we are moving into a world that can be consciously decentralised. A healthy network means you can avoid the bottlenecks of restrictive bank financing or angel investors or acquisition editors or any of the other gatekeepers that emerged out of the legacy, centralised-industrial model. For this larger network/tribe, two things must be kept utmost in mind.

Firstly, a network is *not* a digital asset! You could have the maximum number of friends Facebook allows and still not have a healthy network. Digital platforms facilitate communication within a network. That is all.

---

80   Jocelyn K. Glei. *Maximize Your Potential: Grow Your Expertise, Take Bold Risks & Build an Incredible Career.* Lake Union Publishing, 2013.

You still need to have coffee with people and birthday cards are always appreciated. (June 25, since you asked.)

Secondly, if you are a mechanic, make sure your network consists of more than other mechanics. Have chefs, teachers, painters, waiters, naval officers...whatever. Varied networks provide more useful weak link effects in unpredictable times. I like to think of this as the village in my head. In previous eras you would know your baker or your school teacher; you would know who to speak to about livestock issues or how to fix the roof of your barn. The economics of the modern world make it highly unlikely that you have access to such a variation in skills within easy walking distance. The positive side to the digitisation of networks is that in previous eras, I would not have had an Oxford astrophysicist or a marine biologist in my village...but I do in the village in my head.

A healthy network is one of the best ways to gain exposure to the new economy. Collaboration and shared ownership of income streams are emerging as the new funding model, replacing the old debt-based model of business loans and interest payments. Instead of founding companies, groups and collectives can dynamically appear that share necessary skills or access to potential new markets: don't speak German but have a product or service you wish to market in Germany? Does your network contain any Germans with comparable skills who would be interested in an equity partnership?

In the end, effective networking comes down to a science fiction version of the tribal model. You don't win a mind war on your own.

Wealth in the Medium Term

Even if you happen to be good at making money, you probably aren't good at keeping it. Few people realise this is an entirely separate skill, and it is because of this lack of realisation that most people struggle to retain their wealth. Once it is pointed out, it is obvious. A successful dentist *makes* a lot of money because he or she is good at dentistry. But what do teeth have to do with investing and wealth preservation? Unless your actual job is investment advisor, I am here to tell you that you need to learn a brand new skill.

As you may have guessed from the "Recognising the Bars" chapter, I am a proponent of measuring wealth in terms of their real asset value. Story of my life, but this means inevitably keeping company with some spectacularly weird fringe dwellers. All too often, the words out of somebody's mouth immediately following "physical wealth" have something to do with burying gold coins in your backyard because the US dollar is going to collapse. It isn't. And the gold standard is never coming back. (My guess is we will eventually replace the fiat system with some sort of "basket of commodities" standard administered by the IMF which may or may not include gold.)

What this means is it is useful to be a physical wealth *theorist*, if not a physical wealth *proponent*. We have seen how our crony currency system distorts price signals and interferes with our ability to assess *personal* economic value. It is more difficult for the system to distort the value of the home you were born in or your tribally inherited water access rights as they both have an immovable physicality. In many ways, a preference for physical wealth or investment is philosophical and finds common ground with much of the magical and Pagan communities. For instance, I personally believe permacultural farmland is more valuable than mortgage-backed securities or taxi cab apps, regardless of their relative valuations. Remember the term *humanomics*. You are always in control of what you choose to define as valuable, even if that is nominally measured in currency.

Assuming you plan to remain incarnate for the next twenty years, you will live through the most dramatic changes to the monetary system ever. That makes determining value even more challenging. Historically, when huge monetary changes occur, the best rule of thumb is to control as many real resources as you can. These can include precious metals if you so desire, but it also extends to the above water-rights, energy production systems (solar, geothermal, etc.), and farmland or other arable land. For much of the world, it may be technically safer to keep these assets outside the banking system, especially since widespread policy changes mean you may be forced to bail in your own bank.

In terms of wealth creation strategies, our changing world presents a number of new possibilities. Before we describe them, I cannot stress enough that nothing in this chapter or indeed the entire book constitutes investment advice. The fact that it contains guidelines for a crossroad pact with the devil should really be the giveaway there. Cast your mind back to Deirdre McClosky's notion of the Great Enrichment; the middle classifying of the whole planet. We can observe this process playing out in the world's stock markets. In her 2014 annual wrap up, Catherine Austin Fitts observes that the total value of every stock market on earth in 1990 was $11 trillion dollars.[81] Today it is $70 trillion and is on track for at least $150 trillion as more countries launch their own exchanges and the emerging ones continue to grow. Fitts calls this "a once-in-a-civilisation event," the securitisation of the entire planet. It is a huge growth opportunity and it is presenting itself—indeed is powered by—the increase in access and participation in markets thanks to the rise of mobile and digital communications. We already see the beginnings of this increased participation with the emergence of crowdfunding, micro-funding and investment concepts such as motif investing, where participants can buy trends such as "clean energy" or "America on the move."

As for retirement strategies, the world has changed so much that if you are under forty the social and capital infrastructure, pension funds, and so on will have been largely or completely dismantled by the time you come to retire. There are currently more than $60 trillion in unfunded pension liabilities as we head into the largest mass retirement in human

81   Catherine Austin Fitts. "2014 Annual Wrap Up." Accessed July 5, 2015.
      www.solari.com/blog/wrap-up-ready.

history. Consider the following Ponzi mathemathics, courtesy once again of Charles Hugh-Smith. (Buy his book and subscribe to his blog.)[82]

- 1 retiree consumes the taxes paid by 5 workers.
- Those 5 workers when they retire consume the taxes paid by 25 workers.
- Those 25 workers when they retire consume the taxes paid by 125 workers.
- Those 125 workers when they retire consume the taxes paid by 625 workers.
- Those 625 workers when they retire consume the taxes paid by 3,125 workers.

Superannuation and pension schemes rely on harvesting the wealth of the working age population, "investing it wisely," and paying for the retired members of the schemes with the profits from their canny investments. Don't know about you, but I think I'll pass.

Given the supreme unpredictability facing the economic system, let an understanding of physical wealth inform your retirement decision-making. It is also a very good idea to keep your network healthy as you approach retirement age, a practice that has been humankind's tried and true approach to our later years.

Inevitably, what constitutes wealth and how much of it you actually need to achieve your personal vision of success can only be measured on an individual basis. If there were a defined strategy, everyone would be wealthy. Complicating this further is that the tried and true strategies of the previous five decades are not a good match for the changes the world is currently experiencing. These changes suggest some novel approaches are called for.

---

82   Charles Hugh-Smith. *Get a Job, Build a Career and Defy a Bewildering Economy.* Createspace, 2014.

- **Housing:** Leveraging yourself by more than 300 percent for a single, illiquid asset that has returned less than 1 percent per year over the past fifty years is not a good idea. Take seriously the possibility of multi-generational living or living with a group of friends. This reduces overall financial risk both in terms of debt servicing and any possible job losses; it reduces child care costs, expenses, and it provides alternative vectors for retirement. Why do you think we lived this way for centuries?

- **Geography:** Match your wealth strategy to your location. Rent in areas of high income and high property prices (major cities). Move to areas that present the correct mix of opportunity and cost for you. In short, adapt to your environment. We all know what happens to creatures who don't.

- **Health:** Few people consider their health to be a component of their wealth portfolio, but a bad health diagnosis is the single biggest cause of bankruptcy in America. This has tremendous implications for how you view food spending— it's an *investment*—and should have you thinking extremely seriously about converting parts of your property into food production areas: vegetable plots, aquaponics, etc. Health is absolutely not an area in which to cut costs.

- **Debt and investment:** If you are in debt, consider radical possibilities to get out of it as fast as possible: selling possessions, moving in with friends and family, and so on. Once you are out of debt, *stay out of it*. Debt completely skews your risk profile just as the global economy is undergoing some dramatic changes. Not only does debt increase your overall risk, servicing debt means you are reducing your opportunity to participate in other investments; whether that be your own business, securities and other asset classes, and so on. Never forget that the planet's economy is actually growing, even if the local one is not. Participate!

- **Career:** Make peace with the reality that you will have multiple careers over the course of your lifetime and that there really are no such thing as stable jobs any more. Be prepared to move, be prepared to seize opportunities, and never stop upskilling yourself. If you are debt free and prepared to be geographically dynamic, the world is your oyster.

- **Education:** If someone rich is paying, go expensive. If you are paying, go as cheap as possible. The student with the online degree and a year of interning will always beat the student with a degree from a mid-level college. The difference is so stark that you are probably better off getting into debt to support a year of interning than you are getting a degree. (Not that I would recommend that, of course.) Huge structural changes are looming for the education sector. Think of how angry you will be if you were one of the last students to get so deeply into debt before everything changes.

Finally, there is one other factor to be accounted for in your quest for success. The most important factor…so important it made it into the title of the book.

Chaos

There is the old saying that men plan and God laughs. You will have experienced this in your own life. Success as it transpires has very little to do with planning and very much to do with having a stomach for chaos, for unpredictability. Outside of some highly artificial scenarios such as chess or the more boring sports, the ten thousand hour rule popularised by tobacco lobbyist Malcolm Gladwell has severely limited applicability.

For life's more important goals—making art, finding love—there is neither a minimum or maximum hour rule. Instead you have the permanent state of unpredictability: you probably will not find love tomorrow. This will happen every day until you do.

I say "stomach for" chaos but actually you need to learn to *love* it. If your work life reaches a dead end, dismantle it! If times get tough in your area, assemble a wagon train of friends and family and leave that old life behind for pastures new. If you find yourself in a situation where you are not cultivating rare and valuable skills, walk away. Any of these strategies trigger fear reactions in the majority of the population, but they are already walking casualties in the mind war. You have discovered that not even death can stop you and—armed with spirit allies and ancestors—adventure awaits.

Every strategy and every step on the adventure requires risk. Taking risks is about being brave, not reckless. Fear and victimhood are rejections of risk. They are anti-chaos and pro-status quo. Fear is the first and most important front in the mind war. Pulitzer-nominated journalist John Rappoport says, "Defeat is a program. It's a mind-control program and it is planet-wide." The good news is your finger has been hovering above the off-switch your entire life.

CONCLUSION:
THE TEMPLE AT THE
END OF CAPITALISM

A success magic book is a curious hybrid. It is beyond its scope—and beyond the scope of any book ever written—to declare one is in possession of the meaning of life. (I am afraid you will have to consider that homework.) Similarly, no one explains to you how difficult it is to demonstrate enough personal success to justify taking up the reader's time without sounding like an appalling person in the process. So this has been the most challenging chapter of the book. Figuring that new vistas have a tendency to inspire creativity, I tried writing it all over the world. In the sky over China; in New York's East Village; in Auckland, New Zealand; in South Beach, Miami. I even worked on the bibliography in Rome. (You see what I mean about sounding appalling?) Pieces occurred to me on my journeys, but the overall shape of the chapter remained elusive.

Perhaps flying almost twice around the world in less than a month suggests a shape. Writing this over the Atlantic on the way back to London right now, I am not at the front of the plane, but neither am I at the back. From a coal mining town in regional Australia to an accidental career on the other side of the planet provides interest challenge, globe-trotting excitement... and isn't in banking. For magicians, the answer to the success question cannot be "Hey, let's all be bankers. That will solve everything!" Success comes from suitably incorporating Meaning (with a capital M) into one's life. We require a more sophisticated, more nuanced sense of the term than what is crudely expressed in a bank statement, but we also need to know how those curious glyphs on the bank statement came to be and how they relate to the rest of the world. I am happy that I have enough money to pursue what is important to me in life and grateful that I (currently) enjoy the way I make that money. You can keep your Learjet; I'd rather have a pen and a nice notebook.

The pursuit of Meaning has changed for both the worse and the better in the last two decades. Social mobility may be declining, but creative mobility has never been more achievable. Beginning with the bad news, Meaning is in short supply in our current and medium term socioeconomic future:

- We live in a biosphere undergoing collapse.
- A combination of demographic change and the rise of robotisation do not bode well for the stability of middle-income careers, as growing secular deflation becomes a permanent factor in assessing opportunities for advancement.
- The effect of extreme personal and government debt has yet to be adequately forecast but will have long-term impacts on cultural and social institutions such as healthcare and the arts.

- Crony capitalism: the flagrant manipulation of local and global markets for the sole benefit of a tiny elite at the expense of the rest of us.

- The erosion of civil liberties and the rise of total surveillance means deviations from approved behaviour—an increasingly narrow concept—more and more challenging.

Now to the good news. While we may be living in the last days of centralised capitalism, we also live in an age of wonders. All the greatest novels in western literature can fit on your phone. You can have real-time video conversations with people living in Antarctic research stations at zero cost. Yes, most days the digital world may seem to consist entirely of cat pictures and pornography. But amongst the pussies you can also find the Nag Hammadi library or recordings of Siberian shamans singing to the ancestors. Private space programmes, gay marriage, cameras on mobile handsets that are far more sophisticated than anything I had access to in film school. Would you trade that for a stable, postwar factory job and a house in a racially segregated suburb?

To be clear, this is not a book of digital utopianism. We cannot conclude that you should be happy with your minimum-wage job because at least you have the Internet. Chaos magic first arose into popular consciousness during a time when people believed the digital age presented a future of free expression and fluid identity like some eternal Burning Man. This turned out to be very naïve. I hope I have demonstrated a willingness to stare at what is frankly an extremely challenging incarnation with as little sugarcoating as possible. We will not live happily ever after in the Cloud. However, you can now order seeds for rare, medieval vegetables— far denser in nutrients—and plant them in the backyard of the foreclosed home next door, sharing the bounty with neighbours found via location-based services. You can hear about a genuine Amazonian shaman on Twitter and book the entire journey to meet him or her on a single device while waiting in line for your lunch. You can finally find an audience for your throat-singing albums (probably). The learned networking behaviours of the digital world—such as sharing and mutual interest—are now being taken offline. A digital utopia is only legitimately expressed when you take the best of what it offers to integrate it into your physical existence.

For the first time ever more of us now live in cities than not as a species. Consider the following urban trend: After the Boomers, the next-largest demographic cohort is Generation Y, the so-called Millennials. Far fewer Millennials drive. Far fewer express a desire to live in the suburbs, preferring instead what is known as "urban light" in developer-speak. This means living closer to the centre and existing in walkable spheres of economic influence. It is impossible to overstate or predict the impact of this trend, but I would not want to be the big box retailer at the edge of town in twenty years—I would want to be the independent greengrocer.

A quarter of all people who have ever lived are alive *right now*. In the west at least, this means we are staring at a dramatic cultural change brought about by the first generation to have been raised with a very digital sense of sharing, community, and economies based on networks. The news media paints these changes in a negative light: Millennials live with their parents, Millennials are too coddled to drive, Millennials aren't buying houses. This is the view of their automotive and real estate advertisers, of course, and they *should* be concerned because their world is going away. By 2025, Millenials will make up 75 percent of the workforce. As CEOs and business leaders, they will bring about changes in economic practice as great as the rise of the assembly line or the Internet.

Here is the view of one of the oldest think tanks in Washington, the Brookings Institute:

The desire of Millennials for pragmatic action that brings results will overtake today's emphasis on ideology and polarization as Boomers finally fade from the scene. This cultural shift will be felt in all aspects of the American economy from its marketplaces to its workforce and from its board rooms to the daily decisions of its CEOs.[83]

A three-year study of Millennial attitudes by Accenture found that of their ten least-liked companies, four belonged to the country's most powerful banks: JP Morgan & Chase, Citigroup, Bank of America, and Wells Fargo.[84] But is it really so bad a thing that consumption-based capitalism is ending? As the old world of stable manufacturing jobs shuffles off to retirement with its Boomer devotees, a new world is emerging that is asking the question of what work is for. What will be written on your tombstone? What is it about you that is perishable and what is imperishable? Even if you are not part of the Millennial generation you will still be living in a world built by their hands and their values, and it is *very* different.

Blink and you will miss all of this. It is all too easy to give in to fear and slip back into the control mechanism. That is why the rituals in this book may appear extreme on first read-through. Finding Meaning and success in the post-apocalypse requires a permanent value adjustment. If you picture subjects like wealth, employment, and property ownership as slow-moving planets in an astrological chart, they are currently moving into a new configuration to which we must all respond. It feels counter-intuitive at first, but finding success almost by definition requires you to do the opposite of what everyone else does. It can be so easy to lose your nerve at the last moment and follow the crowd. Crowds cohere around failure, not success. Follow at your peril.

---

83   Morley Winograd and Dr. Michael Hais. "How Millennials Could Upend Wall Street and Corporate America." May 2014. www.brookings.edu//media/research/files /papers/2014/05/millennials%20wall%20st/brookings_winogradv5.pdf.

84   Ibid.

"Degrowth" rather than growth is now the cutting edge of culture. It is a way of being in the world that values access over ownership, that does not measure success or prosperity in terms of consumption. I first moved to London two weeks before Lehmann Brothers collapsed. This was probably the worst time in a thousand years to seek employment in the city. (Although that fire they had a few centuries back probably wasn't great, either.) And so I would apply for open positions in the morning and spend the rest of the day walking the streets and canals, visiting the (free) museums, reading secondhand books in Regent's Park, buying cheap food at markets just as they were closing, watching documentaries online once it got too cold to be outside. I began with more savings than I had ever had before and—because this is how fate works—eventually started my first day of a new job with zero money left in my accounts. I had one pound left and the meal I ate the night before was a supermarket sandwich that cost one pound. It was an awful, stressful time, but it was also somehow wonderful. The experience permanently de-coupled money and status from my sense of personhood or my capacity to appreciate what is actually valuable in human life. You do not need a single cent to your name to appreciate Monet's *Water Lilies* or to pick up a pen and start writing a short story. Today we live in a world where you may ultimately lose your teaching job to a robot, but you have the opportunity for exploration and expression of topics and people that would have got you burned at the stake a few centuries ago.

How you maximise the opportunities presented by our chaotic Kali Yuga is to first become invincible. Your distinct advantage over the majority of the denizens of the west is an unshakeable awareness that the physical realm represents a small sliver in the spectrum of your actual existence. Becoming invincible takes away every map you have ever owned and replaces them all with cold, brilliant freedom. There are no proscribed steps beyond such a point. For example, it is patently impossible to reverse-engineer the decisions I have made into a twenty-point plan to achieve a life that resembles my own … in the vanishingly unlikely scenario that anyone would even want it. Such a plan would not read well: be born in a regional Australian coal mining town, do a film degree, move countries on a whim, spend the next decade making a series of incandescent mistakes, get made redundant fairly consistently … profit. Who needs this? Become invincible and have adventures. The rest is detail.

Since the end of the Great Recession, the amount that the wealth of the 1 percent has grown is greater than the cost of every single social programme in America. We watch the last days of crony capitalism with the same grim fascination that the early gothics observed the cult of the ruin; the centralisation of wealth and power in fewer and fewer hands calls to mind the civilisations that have fallen before our own. Let us return to the Bank of England, one of the epicentres of our current monetary culture. When its surveyor, Sir John Soane, reopened a much-expanded Bank of England fortified against rioting Londoners and doubled in size to accommodate the new force of debt to drive imperial growth, he held an exhibition that showed his gleaming new building in ruins. Even its creator could not look upon the Bank without finding it monstrous and realising it—along with the British Empire—will one day end. (Sir John was pretty much full wizard. Be sure to visit his museum when you are next in London.)

Wizards have always thrived in periods of acute cultural and economic change. Indeed, the western magical tradition as we recognise it today was formed between the first and fourth centuries as empires split in two, new gods arrived from the east, distant provinces were abandoned to their fate, currencies were debased to pay for impossibly large armies, and the libraries of the classical world were scattered to the winds. We appeared again during the economic tumult of the union of Scotland and debt-ridden, Catholic-haunted England under James I—the first and only monarch to write a book on witch-hunting and demonology. We appeared again in the cane and cotton fields of the New World where merchants became richer than kings while humans were kept as property. We wait in the shadows for things to get rough and then step into the light like smiling loan sharks.

To do what, exactly? Inevitably, a regime of practical enchantment is judged on the physical results it manifests. I do not shy away from this. Success magic should bring you success. If not, you are doing it wrong. We cannot make success be whatever you want it to be lest we rob the term of its usefulness. What, then, does success look like in a world where the previous yardsticks—expensive cars, suburban houses—are no longer relevant? What are the outward manifestations of a meaningful, magical life? Success is not a McMansion in negative equity. Success is camping in a Languedoc field for a summer, drinking pastis and playing boules with the locals. Success is getting someone to buy one of your paintings, even if it is for a dollar. Success is extracting sufficient wealth from a dysfunctional system without the status anxiety that so often accompanies it.

Ultimately, success is a head game. It is bringing your best army to the mind war. Decades of happiness research have revealed that employment is poorly suited to making you happy and that, in fact, humans are extremely bad at predicting what will make us happy in the first place. Somewhere in the nascent science of consciousness research and how our minds interact with the physical world is the secret the hermeticists and yogis of the past seek to impart to us from beyond the grave. At some fundamental level you are creating and changing the universe. Practical magic can only amplify this pre-existing function. It cannot even supply the wisdom to know when to use it and when to hold off. Such wisdom is hard won and only arrives after many campaigns. You will recognise its arrival when your creative, imaginal capacity knows when to change the changeable and when to find another way around the unchangeable.

Success is being satisfied with an outcome you set out to achieve. Stop at nothing and you will eventually get there. Welcome to the Kali Yuga. Happy hunting.

APPENDIX:
THE GRIMOIRE THAT WASN'T

You may have noticed that books on magick, however interesting they are,
eventually get onto boring exercises which apparently you have to do every
day in order to actually get on to the interesting magickal heights scaled by
the experts. They're usually authoritarian about it, and the exercises tend to
be deadly dull. They nearly put me off magick for life!

———

GENESIS BREYER P-ORRIDGE

In the extremely unlikely scenario in which this is the first magic book you
have ever picked up, common courtesy dictates I offer you some baseline
magical skills and spells. This presents a number of problems in our post-
Internet world.

Firstly, yes, you probably should do nothing but twenty minutes of
daily meditation every day for six months before you start enchanting.
You won't, however. I certainly didn't. It took me more than ten years to
begrudgingly admit to myself that meditation is the single best thing you
can do to improve your health and your magic and that I should probably
do more of it. Your mileage will not vary much, that I promise.

Secondly, I am innately suspicious of any sort of list of baseline practices because it can resemble, in the mind of the reader, a training course. Disavow yourself of this notion immediately. I am not a teacher, I am a sharer. Also, if you *do* happen to be new to magic, you will skip over all the beginning stuff and jump straight to the demonology anyway. As a teenager, I leapt with youthful confidence over all Aleister Crowley's boring, dreary chapters on yoga and went straight to the bits about drugs, sex, and demons. It would be churlish to deny you the same misadventure (which it most certainly is).

Finally, the role of the grimoire or book of shadows has not only changed in our post-digital age, it has also had new light shed upon it by the very existence of the Internet. If you read the works of Jake Stratton-Kent or Owen Davies, you will see that grimoires and other magical texts are necessarily incomplete, appear in different versions, are translated with varying degrees of accuracy, swap the gender of some of their principal spirits, etc. There are no definitive, dusty tomes come down to us from hoary antiquity that tell us this is How Magic Works. In all cases it is someone's best guess, it is the personal workbook of a particular person at a particular time … the spirits and incantations that he or she found to be efficacious. In point of fact, it is this very custom of individual collation that *is* the western tradition. As Hans Dieter Betz points out in the introduction to his definitive *Greek Magical Papyri*, the magicians of the late Hellenic world were wandering craftsmen and women, picking up spells and hymns that appeared useful. They no longer understood the meter of the incantations, they bundled together gods, goddesses and angels, they blurred the nature and pronunciation of the spirits. The whole thing is a mess. A delicious, chaotic mess. Our magical ancestors forever tested new formulae and invocations, retaining only those that worked for them. Thus was born the western magical tradition.

We have an even greater opportunity to hybridise our working than even those magicians working at the end of the Roman empire. Today we have newly translated Akkadian and Sumerian texts appearing on university websites every day, online botanicas that ship worldwide, and we have an explosion of practitioners publishing their own experiments and findings on thousands of blogs and websites around the planet. Whilst it is true that any half-decent magician could lay waste to entire economies with just Paul Huson's *Mastering Witchcraft* or the Simon *Necronomicon,* today we can and do drink from the firehose of practical magic.

And so it is in the spirit of our magical forebears that I present a collection of personal practical enchantments focused on success magic. This is not my Book of Shadows; I possess no such object. These are merely a few gulps from a firehose that has been left running for millennia. Drink, then contribute.

Meditation

Forgive the arrogance of attempting to summarise mankind's most important consciousness technology in a few words, but here we go.

1. Sit comfortably, do not lie down.

2. Focus on your breath: in through the nose, out through the mouth. Breathe in, then hold, then out, then hold, all for the same length of time.

3. When your mind wanders onto other thoughts, as surely it will, gently bring it back to the focus on the breath.

That's it. Do it daily, even if just for ninety seconds to start with. We are coming up on about three decades of medical and scientific research that suggests mindfulness meditation has a miraculous cascade effect on your entire body. It can reduce or completely cure depression, it improves metabolism, it lengthens your telomeres. If there was any way big pharma could turn this into a pill, meditation would be declared a more significant medical discovery than antibiotics.

Successful people meditate. Do it.

The Chaosphere

Consider this a chaos magic equivalent of chakras, which I also work with. The chaosphere, however, is more interoperable with more magical paths and can also function as an instant protective barrier in psychically uncomfortable situations. Chakras are nevertheless worth investigating too. (That's what the Internet is for.) The chaosphere is based on a ritual first designed by the English artist and grandfather of chaos magic Austin Osman Spare by way of Stephen Mace's excellent *Stealing Fire From Heaven*. Modifications and mistakes are my own.

1. Close your eyes and imagine a line of brilliant white light extending down from the heavens, through the top of your head right through the point of view between your eyes.

2. Vibrate "Baph—o—met" as you do so.

3. With them still closed, picture a brilliant point of light floating about two feet in front of your eyes, like an angry, cold Tinkerbell.

4. Picture this point of light orbit around your head and then spiral down to below your feet, forming an iridescent sphere.

5. Have the point of light perform the same function, starting at your feet, running up behind you, over your head, and back down to your feet, forming a second sphere. (I personally picture this happening six times so I can keep track of it like a clock face.)

6. Picture the column of light descending from the heavens "landing" inside the sphere and begin to expand until the entire sphere is filled with purple-inflected white light.

7. Say words to the effect of the litany from the notorious Mass of Chaos B:

> *In the first aeon, I was the Great Spirit.*
>
> *In the second aeon, Men knew me as the Horned God, Pangenitor Panphage.*
>
> *In the third aeon, I was the Dark one, the devil.*
>
> *In the fourth aeon, Men knew me not for I am the Hidden One.*
>
> *In this new aeon, I appear before you as Baphomet.*
>
> *The God before all gods who shall endure to the ends of the earth.*

8. Take several deep breaths and feel the glowing sphere solidify, then vibrate "baph—o—met" once more and picture eight pleasingly steampunk arrows jutting out of your sphere.

A Universal Conjuration

One inevitably lands on a preferred go-to conjuration after taking a few of them for a spin. The *Prayer of the Salamanders* seems particularly popular. It is certainly quite evocative, but I prefer the faintly shamanic undertones of the Harleianus 5596 *Magical Treatise of Solomon*, albeit with a few modifications I commend to you below.

> *I conjure you, oh spirit(s), by God, whom the Angels, Archangels, Principalities, Thrones, Dominations, the Cherubim and the full eyes of the Seraphim, Virtues and Powers are serving and not ceasing to cry and say "Holy, holy, holy Lord Sabaoth, the heaven and earth are full of thy glory."*

I conjure you, spirit(s), by the heaven and the earth and the
holy mysteries of God. I conjure you, spirit(s), by the seven planets
of heaven, wherever you may be, come to me at once, without
delay. I conjure you by the air, the fire, the waters, the earth, by
the sea and the rivers, wherever you may be, whether in heaven or
under the earth, in a mountain, a hill, a plain, an open sea, a lake,
far or close; wherever you may be and wherever you may dwell,
come here without delay.[85]

I have used this to great success with your classic goetic spirits but also in what we might cheekily call "archaeological magic"—summoning spirits from barrows and calling upon spirits of place. It has the benefit of being among the least-bullying or hectoring conjurations found in the grimoires. Typically they are far less polite. You catch more spirits with honey. (This is both literally and metaphorically true, incidentally.)

Saint Columba's Prayer for Victory

Saint Columba was one of the first—if not the first—spiritual teachers to introduce Christianity to mainland Britain from Ireland. Modern Paganism has laboured under a very poor reading of history that would consider this wholly negative. If you have ever visited Iona in the off-season, you will see just how difficult a task Columba set himself. In the intervening centuries, his story has accumulated all manner of folk customs and tales that paint him as the archetypal wizard: dealings with kings, having magic battles with Pagans, brokering wars and marriages, protecting the innocent, curing livestock, flying through the air, and so on. He has even ended up with a few titles that point to his involvement—posthumous or not—with the fairy folk such as "Columba of the Graves and Tombs."

---

85   Ioannis Marathakis. *The Magical Treatise of Solomon, or Hygromanteia.* Golden
      Hoard Press, 2012.

What needs to be borne in mind is that many of these instances of religious conversion relied on the incomers having better magic than the incumbent priesthood. Columba convincingly won. Think of him as Gandalf in a purple cloak.

> *Mouth of the dumb,*
> *Light of the blind,*
> *Foot of the lame,*
> *To the fallen stretch out your hand.*
>
> *Strengthen the senseless,*
> *Restore the mad.*
>
> *O Columba, hope of the Scots,*
> *By your merits' mediation,*
> *Make us companions,*
> *Of the blessed angels.*
>
> *By the blood of our Lord Jesus Christ,*
> *Grant us the Victory that God alone can bestow.*
>
> *Amen.*[86]

An Adaptive Consecration

This is a fairly simple but potent charm for consecrating objects to be used in ritual, modified from José Leitão's *The Book of St. Cyprian*. Make the sign of the cross at each +.

Agla + On + Tetragrammaton + Abraxas per dominum nostrum + fiat-Deus luxunus + in tenebris-trinus +.

---

86   Geoff Holder. *Guide to Mysterious Iona (Mysterious Scotland)*. The History
      Press, 2007.

Restricting Anger

Unless it is just my abrasive personality, it appears to me that we have a tendency to underestimate the impact of gossip and petty-mindedness on our careers, even if we are unaware it is going on. (Tip: It is always going on.) If you happen to live near a botanica, there are any number of anti-gossip candles and charms you may find useful. Fire seems to suit these kinds of workings. *Sans* candle vendors, here is an adaptation from the Greek Magical Papyri:

1. If you have a particular person you would like to bind, write their name on a piece of paper. If not, leave it blank.

2. Write "CHNEŌM" diagonally across the name, then fold the paper in half.

3. Light a candle or stand in front of an open fire of some sort and say the following:

   I restrain the anger and gossip of all,
   especially of (name), which is CHNEŌM.

4. Burn the paper in the candle flame or throw it in the fire.

Banishing and Protection

It will surprise you just how many supermarket spices are efficacious in magic, particularly protection and exorcism. Simply burning asafoetida on a charcoal briquette and walking room to room will remove all but the most potent negative spirit influences. (It will also clear your home of humans too, because it completely stinks. Maybe file that away for the next time you throw a dinner party that goes on too long.)

Another folk magical practice I have found to be useful is to plant rosemary in your yard to prevent hauntings. If you are going to pursue necromancy in any serious way, it is nice to have an "always on" solution. Pour some red wine over your rosemary bush on St. John's Eve as a traditional thank you.

My go-to protection amulet, which can be worn, placed under the bed, above doors, etc, comes from the Nordic *svarteboken* tradition. Although this one is from Denmark, it is a continuation of an amulet-manufacture tradition that dates back to the classical world, if not before. Namely, the inscribing of a magical word repeated on each line with diminishing letters. This one is known as the Kalemaris. Write it on paper, carve it into wood, pipe it onto pastry. Up to you.

KALEMARIS
KALEMARI
KALEMAR
KALEMA
KALEM
KALE
KAL
KA
K

For further information or assistance with protective magic, Jason Miller has written the definitive book on the subject: *Protection and Reversal Magick*. Highly recommended.

City Spirits

This presumes you actually live in a city, of course. As previously mentioned, for the first time in history more of us do than don't, so it is a good bet. City spirits are more complex than, say, waterfall spirits. It is rare for waterfalls to declare war, invent democracy, or unleash fractional reserve banking on the world.

The bigger or older the city, the less it is influenced by offerings. London, for instance, merely expects them the way an absolute monarch expects tribute. Your offerings will not change its mind should it wish to crush you. (The Thames is more amenable to offerings if you happen to live in town. They have a "good cop/bad cop" thing going on.) Consider the offerings as a cover charge rather than a transaction. Your ability to achieve success or wealth or love or whatever will rely in no small part on the location you have selected. This payment merely gets you through the door.

If you are honest with yourself, you already know where your city spirit is most easily found. It is the place where you feel the most "London-ness" or "Chicago-ness," etc. As for offerings, many of the common suggestions—feeding the homeless, volunteering at a shelter—are not going to move the needle very much with city spirits and indicate a very poor understanding of the history of urbanisation. There are certainly many fine reasons for volunteering at a foodbank, but if the spirit of London cared about homelessness I would not walk past so many people sleeping rough in Soho on my way to work. Should you still wish to use service as an offering then volunteer at a graveyard or assist the dead in some way. For whatever reason, city spirits care more for their dead than they do for their homeless. (A working hypothesis here would be that a city spirit is at least partly composed of the dead it contains.)

More direct, physical offerings are appropriate. I throw coins in the Thames as offerings, largely because I find it pleasing to realise the Romans did the exact same thing almost two thousand years ago. But you can even do something as simple as pouring out some of your drink (the first part of your drink!) in a park during your lunch break. Coins in fountains are also good. Whatever you choose, consider a ritual shape similar to this:

1. Sit or stand somewhere that feels very "of the place," with your offering held in your hands.

2. Mentally reach out for at least a few blocks in every direction around you, calling on the spirit of place.

3. Rapidly collapse your attention back from all these directions toward the offering in your hands, then pour it out, throw it in the river, etc.

4. Repeat reasonably often.

Emergency Flashlight

The second time I was fired/performance-managed out of a job was the worst so far. I had only recently moved to New Zealand and was working at a fashion retailer. The new store manager loathed me on first sight and made it her mission to remove me. I was offered the usual things like union or legal representation for the performance meetings, all of which I refused because I had two things going for me: the unshakeable self-confidence of youth and an impenetrable force field. I have retained only one of them. During what was a frankly very hostile meeting, the company HR director said he had never seen anyone handle this type of meeting quite so well. But of course. Genuinely none of their hostility was getting through the force field. Inside the bubble it felt like a dispassionate business discussion.

Life in general and business in particular is a veritable rat king of sudden nastiness, ulterior motives, and manipulation. You will never find a "clean" game for the same reason you will never find warm snow. The conditions of reality simply do not allow for it to exist. This is why you need a magical emergency flashlight. In many respects, this technique is a companion to the chaosphere because it is a method of instantly switching it on in those unexpected moments. Mine takes its inspiration from *The Lord of the Rings*, which will come as no surprise to those of you familiar with my blog. You will recall the part in the third film (which is actually in the second book) where Frodo uses the vial of water given to him by Galadriel to briefly banish the giant spider, Shelob. He says a few words and the water inside begins to glow, sending the spider packing. These are the words he says:

Aiya Eärendil Elenion Ancalima!

Before you dismiss the idea of using fictional enchantments as so much 1990s chaos magic claptrap, let's consider the origin of the phrase. In Tolkien's mythology, Eärendil was an Elvish mariner who sailed the night sky with a jewel known as a Silmaril. He is Middle Earth's Evening Star, i.e., Venus. The name comes from an obscure Old English angelic name, *Earendel*, meaning "star dawn." Professor Tolkien found the name in an anonymously written ninth-century poem, *Crist I*:

> *Hail Earendel, brightest of Angels!*
> *Above Middle Earth, sent unto Men.*

So the real version of Eärendil is an angel, the Morning Star—and thus remains Venus—and is also John the Baptist in the context of the original poem as Venus heralds the rising of the Sun/Son. That is quite a lot of punch in a single line of a made-up language! Plus you have a handy visual reference in your film collection should you need it.

Memorise the phrase and visualise the blinding, protective white light of the Silmaril emanating out from your heart centre. It can be used when encountering unexpected hostility or negativity or any situation that doesn't allow for a lengthier ritual response. I use it on some sections of the tube where the line runs through old plague pits, for instance. Try it out. Practice makes awesome.

Annunaki Godform Assumption

This technique I commend to you *reservedly*. It almost did not make it into the final draft because it is, without question, the most dangerous technique in the book. But it is hugely effective if you have the stomach for it. Two pieces of context are necessary before we continue.

The modern western practice of assuming godforms originates with the Golden Dawn and is in and of itself a very worthwhile activity to explore. Briefly, you learn as much as you can about the attributes and mythologies of a particular god/dess, fill a ritual space with objects, colours, and smells associated with the god/dess and then sit there visualising yourself transforming into this being. Think of it like cosmic theatre sports.

Secondly, when I say "annunaki," I do not mean the actual beings from Sumerian mythology. I mean the beings posited by ancient aliens theorist Zechariah Sitchin. I mean the space lizards who came to earth on nuclear powered rocket ships and genetically engineered mankind to mine gold to shore up the atmosphere of their home planet before getting into a nuclear war with each other, appointing some bloodline families to rule on their behalf and then leaving again.

To put it mildly, this is an extremely unlikely historical scenario. And by that I mean it emphatically did not happen. But after the last thirty years of alternative archaeological books and television programmes we all have a very vivid mental image of the "gods as hostile aliens" motif. It has spun off into about a dozen reptilian overlord conspiracy theories to boot. So, several years ago, after largely confining myself to western Europe for about five years, I was suddenly flying all over the world. New York, Fiji, Los Angeles, Hamburg, Tuscany, etc. It was the Fiji leg in particular that got me thinking about a potential godform experiment. It is one of those holiday destinations where the staff are so deferential it makes you feel awkward. They all but bow as you walk past. Tropical island holidays tend to be things of almost obscene luxury, especially given that they invariably happen in countries with few other viable economic sectors. It is not hard to imagine that if the planet were ruled by hostile alien overlords this is how they would live.

In this case, begin the godform assumption when you are on an airplane as it begins to speed up and take off. Picture your hands and feet morphing into three-taloned claws, your second set of eyelids blinking, your height extending by several feet, and allow a cold, calculating, uncaring personality to arise... like you are being dispatched to sort of a recalcitrant province of disposable ape men. Become an interloping Lord of the Earth.

It all seems fairly innocuous until you try it. The assumption triggers in me a metallic, influenza taste in my mouth that is my indicator I have wandered into a less salubrious corner of the imaginal realm. Retain this impression until about cruising altitude and then let it melt into the background. (For some reason this works better for me on take-off rather than landing. But I am usually pretty drunk by the time we land.) The personality change is remarkable, particularly in someone who is not overly misanthropic. No, really. And I will just add that it was a mere several months—perhaps six flights in all—of trialling this assumption before the startup I was working for was acquired by a large, publicly listed media company, netting me the single biggest windfall of my life so far.

Abre Camino

On the blog, I once asked whether a road opener was the only spell you needed. The question relates back to Nassim Taleb's concept of optionality and seizing opportunities. What is a love spell but a request for new romantic roads to be opened? What about job-hunting spells?

Abre camino candles, incense, and oils are the ones I most often have to hand. I use abre camino oil when consecrating new statues, to open the road for a spirit to indwell in it. The incense also gets used fairly often when shoaling sigils.

An open road is a road devoid of obstacles. Viewed from this perspective, you could almost say Ganesha is the only success god you need. As such, it is worth considering 108 recitations of OM GUM GANAPATI-YEH NAMAHA as a cheeky auditory equivalent of a road opener. YouTube will assist you with proper pronunciation.

Powerful Spell of the Bear

Another victory spell, this time from the Greek Magical Papyri.

1. In the evening, arrange a table with seven tealight candles and a small offering bowl of cumin seeds and honey.

2. Use your Night Sky app to arrange the table facing Ursa Major (effectively facing north).

3. Write the following on a piece of paper and have it to hand. This is the hundred-lettered name of Typhon.

ACHCHŌR ACHCHŌR ACHACHACHPTOUMI
CHACHCHŌ CHARACHŌCH CHAPTOUMĒ
CHŌRA CHŌCH APTOUMIMĒ CHŌCHAPTOU
CHARACHPTOU CHACHCHŌ CHARA
CHŌCH PTENACHŌCHEOU

4. Light the candles, then recite the following, preferably while holding an Egyptian walking onion, if you can find one.

I call upon you, holy, very-powerful, very-glorious, very-strong, holy, autochthons, assistants of the great god, the powerful chief daimons, you who are inhabitants of Chaos, of Erebos, of the abyss, of the depth, of earth, dwelling in the recesses of heaven, lurking in the nooks and crannies of houses, shrouded in dark clouds, watchers of things not to be seen, guardians of secrets, leaders of those in the underworld, administrators of the infinite, wielding power over earth, earth-shakers, foundation-layers, servants in the chasm, shudderful fighters, fearful ministers, turning the spindle, freezing snow and rain, air transversers, wind-bringers, lords of Fate, inhabitants of dark Erebos, bringers of compulsion, sending flames of fire, bringing snow and dew, wind-releasers, disturbers of the deep, treaders on the calm sea, mighty in courage, grievers of the heart, powerful

potentates, cliff-walkers, adverse daimons, iron hearted,
wild-tempered, unruly, guarding Tartaros, misleading
Fate, all-seeing, all-hearing, all-subjecting, heaven-walkers,
spirit-givers, living simply, heaven-shakers, gladdening the
heart, those who join together death, revealers of angels,
punishers of mortals, sunless revealers, rulers of daimons,
almighty, holy unconquerable AŌTH ABAŌTH BASYM
ISAK SABAŌTH IAŌ IAKŌP MANARA SKORTOURI
MOTROUM EPHRAULA THREERSA[87]

Then describe what you wish the spirits to achieve for you. Once you have done this, take the hundred-lettered name of Typhon and burn it in the candles. Attempt to have it burned by all seven of the candles and have the ash drop in the bowl with the cumin and honey.

Dreaming

Followers of the blog will know that I have been banging the drum for intermittent fasting for years. Initially embarked upon for a weight management solution that can fit a lifestyle of someone working in food media, one of the immediate discoveries was just how potent your dreams are on fast days. They are so vivid they border on entheogenic.

Here is what Peter Grey wrote about dreaming in our modern world in *Apocalyptic Witchcraft*:

If there can be a war on dreaming, I propose a devastating counter-strike.

Recognise that something sinister has been sculpting the landscape of dream. We are seeing an unprecedented colonisation and colonialisation of the dream worlds. When we discussed incubation it

---

87   Hans Dieter Betz. *The Greek Magical Papyri in Translation Including the Demotic Spells. Second Edition.* University of Chicago Press, 1997.

was made clear that the Ancient World understood the importance of dream, and since then it has been accumulating grey silt. The dream world is becoming as polluted as the natural world, as despoiled. Before we even reach the Asclepium, our minds are chorusing with chatter, assailed by demands. The previous strategy of thou shalt not have unauthorised dreams *has been superceded by a more terrible strategy. It is not simply dream which is derided as meaningless, but every aspect of our lives. In a parody of Hassan I Sabbah, nothing is true and thus nothing is permitted. We parade our inner selves which are revealed to be no more than loyalty to a sect of compatible brands. When we see ourselves and the world around us we do not recognise the sacred. Our culture has devoured itself.*[88]

Dreaming is a cornerstone magical practice the world over. It is the commonest route into the spirit world. Yet today we go to sleep filled with artificial foods, with a carcinogenic cellular device less than a foot from our heads, surrounded by WiFi signals and devices whose lights never seem to turn off. One way or the other, you must take back your own dream state. This involves:

- Keeping your mobile phone far away from you and returning to an old-timey alarm clock.

- Ensure your bedroom is properly dark: i.e., decent curtains and no electrical devices such as laptops that all seem to have at least three lights you can never turn off. (Note: this will also make you live longer, apparently.)

- Fasting. It has been an essential mystical process for centuries. You simply won't believe me until you try it. As with the below suggestion, always check that fasting is not

---

88 Peter Grey. *Apocalyptic Witchcraft.* Scarlet Imprint, 2013.

contraindicated for a particular medication or condition (such as pregnancy).

- Herbal allies: Valerian root tea, mugwort tea, or a tincture of Egyptian blue lotus are all worthwhile, legal herbal supplements to try just before bed. Be especially careful with the first two and any medication you are on that affect the liver. Definitely do not go anywhere near mugwort if you are pregnant.

In many ways, dreaming is an excellent place to end this appendix as it interfaces with all the enchantments not only in this chapter but throughout the whole book. Having the cleanest route possible into the dream realm is essential for spirit guidance and inspiration in response to a particular working or ritual. New spirits, gods, allies, and possibilities will also present themselves to you. Properly activated, your dreaming is one heck of a strategic advantage in achieving your dreams. Go to.

BIBLIOGRAPHY

Adams, Cameron, David Luke, Anna Waldstein, Ben Sessa, and David King (editors). *Breaking Convention: Essays on Psychedelic Consciousness*. London: Strange Attractor Press, 2013.

Ariely, Dan. *The Upside of Irrationality*. London: HarperCollins, 2010.

Athanassakis, Apostolos N., and Benjamin M. Wolkow. *The Orphic Hymns*. Baltimore: Johns Hopkins University Press, 2013.

Baker, Jim. *The Cunning Man's Handbook*. London: Avalonia, 2014.

Betz, Hans Dieter. *The Greek Magical Papyri in Translation*. London: University of Chicago Press, 1996.

Brooks, Michael. *At the Edge of Uncertainty*. London: Profile Books, 2014.

Brooks, Michael. *13 Things That Don't Make Sense*. London: Profile Books, 2009.

Carroll, Peter J., and Matt Kaybryn. *Epoch: The Esotericon & Portals of Chaos*. Bristol: Kingsown Publishers, 2014.

Carroll, Peter J. *The Apophenion: A Chaos Magic Paradigm*. Oxford: Mandrake of Oxford, 2008.

———. *Liber Kaos*. York Beach, ME: Samuel Weiser, 1992.

———. *Liber Null & Psychonaut*. York Beach: Samuel Weiser, 1987.

———. *The Octavo (Roundworld Edition): A Sorcerer-Scientist's Grimoire*. Oxford: Mandrake of Oxford, 2011.

Carter, Chris. *Science and Psychic Phenomena*. Rochester, VT: Inner Traditions, 2012.

Crowley, Aleister. *The Book of Thoth*. York Beach, ME: Samuel Weiser, 1996.

D'Alessandro, David F. *Career Warfare*. New York: McGraw Hill, 2004.

Davies, Owen. *Grimoires: A History of Magic Books*. Oxford, UK: Oxford University Press, 2009.

Forbes, Steve, and Elizabeth Ames. *Money: How the Destruction of the Dollar Threatens the Global Economy and What We Can Do About It*. New York: McGraw-Hill Education, 2014. Kindle edition.

Gimian, James, and Barry Boyce. *The Rules of Victory: Strategies from the Art of War*. Boston: Shambhala Publications, 2008.

Glei, Jocelyn K. *Maximize Your Potential: Grow Your Expertise, Take Bold Risks & Build an Incredible Career*. Seattle: Lake Union Publishing, 2013. Kindle edition.

Godin, Seth. *Linchpin: Are You Indispensable?* London: Piatkus, 2010.

———. *The Dip*. New York: Penguin, 2007.

Grey, Peter. *Apocalyptic Witchcraft*. London: Scarlet Imprint, 2013.

Hansen, George P. *The Trickster and the Paranormal.* Bloomington, IN: Xlibris, 2001. Kindle edition.

Harpur, Patrick. *The Philosopher's Secret Fire.* Glastonbury, UK: Squeeze Press, 2009.

Hillman, D. C. A. *The Chemical Muse: Drug Use and the Roots of Western Civilization.* New York: Thomas Dunne Books, 2008.

Holder, Geoff. *The Guide to Mysterious Iona and Staffa.* Stroud: Tempus Publishing. 2007.

Hugh-Smith, Charles. *Get a Job, Build a Real Career, Defy a Bewildering Economy.* Berkeley, CA: Oftwominds.com, 2014.

Huson, Paul. *The Devil's Picturebook.* London: Sphere Books, 1972.

———. *Mastering Witchcraft.* New York: Perigree Books, 1980.

———. *The Mystical Origins of the Tarot.* Rochester, VT: Destiny Books, 2004. Kindle edition.

Hutton, Ronald. *The Triumph of the Moon: A History of Modern Pagan Witchcraft.* Oxford: Oxford University Press, 1999.

Hyatt, Christopher S., and S. Jason Black. *Pacts with the Devil.* Tempe, AZ: New Falcon Publications, 1993.

Jodorowsky, Alejandro. *Manual of Psychomagic: The Practice of Shamanic Psychotherapy.* Rochester, VT: Inner Traditions, 2015.

Johnston, Sarah Iles. *Restless Dead: Encounters Between the Living and the Dead in Ancient Greece.* London: University of California Press, 2013.

Jünger, Ernst. *The Forest Passage.* New York: Telos Press, 2013.

Kastrup, Bernardo. *Why Materialism Is Baloney.* Alresford, UK: Iff Books, 2014.

Kay, John. *Obliquity: Why Our Goals Are Best Achieved Indirectly.* London: Profile Books, 2010.

Kripal, Jeffrey J. *Authors of the Impossible.* Chicago: University of Chicago Press, 2010.

Leitão, José. *The Book of St. Cyprian: The Sorcerer's Treasure.* Yorkshire, UK: Hadean Press, 2014.

Levenda, Peter. *The Dark Lord.* Lake Worth, FL: Ibis Press, 2013.

Mace, Stephen. *Stealing the Fire from Heaven.* Phoenix, AZ: Dagon Productions, 2003.

Marathakis, Ioannis. *The Magical Treatise of Solomon, or Hygromanteia.* Singapore: Golden Hoard Press, 2011.

McKenna, Terence. *The Archaic Revival.* New York: HarperOne, 1991.

———. *True Hallucinations.* New York: Harper Collins, 1994.

Meyer, Marvin W. *The Ancient Mysteries: A Sourcebook.* San Francisco: Harper & Row, 1987.

Mishev, Georgi. *Thracian Magic, Past and Present: The Folklore and Magical Practices of the Balkan Peninsula.* London: Avalonia, 2012. Kindle edition.

Mlodinow, Leonard. *The Drunkard's Walk: How Randomness Rules Our Lives.* London: Penguin, 2009.

Piketty, Thomas. *Capital in the Twenty-First Century.* New York: Harvard University Press, 2014.

Radin, Dean. *The Noetic Universe: The Scientific Evidence for Psychic Phenomena.* London: Random House, 2009.

Robbins, Tony. *Money: Master the Game.* London: Simon & Schuster, 2014.

Roney-Dougal, Serena. *The Faery Faith: An Integration of Science with Spirit*. London: Green Magic, 2003.

Ruck, Carl A. P., and Mark A. Hoffman. *Entheogens, Myth and Human Consciousness*. Oakland, CA: Ronin Publishing, 2013.

Sheldrake, Rupert. *The Science Delusion*. London: Coronet, 2012. Kindle edition.

Skinner, Stephen, and David Rankine. *The Keys to the Gateways of Magic: Summoning the Solomonic Archangels and Demon Princes*. London: Golden Hoard Press, 2005.

Solomon, Grant, and Jane Solomon. *The Scole Experiments: Scientific Evidence for Life After Death*. London: Judy Piatkus Ltd., 2000.

Stratton-Kent, Jake. *The Headless One*. Yorkshire, UK: Hadean Press, 2015. Smashwords edition.

———. *The Testament of St. Cyprian the Mage*. London: Scarlet Imprint, 2014.

———. *The True Grimoire*. London: Scarlet Imprint, 2009.

Taleb, Nassim Nicholas. *Antifragile*. London: Penguin, 2012.

Targ, Russell. *The Reality of ESP: A Physicist's Proof of Psychic Abilities*. Wheaton, IL: Quest Books, 2012.

Templar, Richard. *The Rules of Management*. Upper Saddle River, NJ: Pearson Education, 2005.

———. *The Rules of Work*. Upper Saddle River, NJ: Pearson Education, 2003.

Turk, James, and John Rubino. *The Money Bubble*. Online: Dollar Collapse Press, 2013.

Vallee, Jacques. *Dimensions: A Casebook of Alien Contact*. London: Souvenir Press, 1988.

Vallee, Jacques, and Chris Aubeck. *Wonders in the Sky*. London: Tarcher/Penguin, 2010.

Vallee, Jacques, and Janine Vallee. *Challenge to Science: The UFO Enigma*. New York: Ballatine Books, 1977.

Van Lommel, Pim. *Consciousness Beyond Life: The Science of the Near-Death Experience*. London: Harper Collins eBooks, 2010. Kindle edition.

White, David Gordon. *Myths of the Dog-Man*. London: University of Chicago Press, 1991.

INDEX

D

decans, 88

decapitation, 65

decentralisation, 26

Dee, John, 149

deficit, 17, 18

defixiones, 128

deflation, 19, 30, 180

degrowth, 184

delphi, 103

democracy, 195

demographics, 35, 37

demon, 46

demonic, 146

demonology, 185, 188

demons, 4, 11, 61, 188

demotic, 93, 202

Denmark, 195

depatterning, 64

derivatives, 21, 22

Detroit, 20

devil, 101, 103, 104, 106, 107, 148,
 160, 174, 191

directionality, 66

discoverie of witchcraft, 78

divination, 46, 113–118, 120,
 123, 124, 126, 135

dog, 34, 88, 89, 91

dogs, 88–91

Roney-Dougal, Serena, 98

dreams, 11, 52, 72, 149, 152,
 202–204

drug, 62

E

earendel, 198

Egypt, 65, 66, 88–90, 112, 128

Egyptian, 47, 66, 87, 88, 90, 201,
 204

Einkorn, 61

electron, 48, 49

employment, 4, 20, 36, 38, 39, 41,
 54, 147, 148, 160, 163, 183,
 184, 186

enchantment, 7, 51, 56, 68, 69, 76,
 102, 108, 126, 128, 129, 131,
 135, 148, 186

England, 15, 82, 185

enoch, 140

entheogenic, 202

entheogens, 142

equities, 12, 30

equity, 172, 186

Eurasia, 16

Europe, 14, 16, 25, 36, 37, 96,
 103, 112, 148, 161, 199

Greenspan, 34

grimoire, 50, 106, 128, 187, 188

grimoires, 66, 78, 188, 192

H

hagiography, 78, 88

Nag Hammadi, 181

headless, 65, 67–70, 92, 125

headlessness, 65

healthcare, 32, 35, 36, 39, 40, 180

Hebrew, 65, 112

Heisenberg, 50

Heliopolis, 94

hell, 21, 93, 103

Hellenic, 66, 188

Hellenistic, 90

Hermanubis, 87–95, 106, 107

Hermes, 55, 87, 88, 90–92, 99–101, 103, 106, 107

Hermetica, 56

hologram, 43, 45, 55, 56

holographic, 2, 45, 56

Hoodoo, 137

horoscope, 118–120

housing, 16, 20, 21, 23, 24, 26, 30, 34, 35, 40, 53, 148, 154, 157, 159, 166, 176

humanomics, 10, 12, 173

Huson, Paul, 63, 64, 112, 189

hygromanteia, 140, 192

I

iao, 95, 125

idolatry, 103, 104

incantation, 63, 79

incantations, 188

incarnation, 1, 3, 123, 155, 167, 181

incense, 68, 92, 108, 125, 128, 138, 200

income, 26–28, 30, 32–34, 153–156, 162, 164, 165, 172, 176

India, 16, 89

Indra, 56

Indus, 12

inflation, 11, 15, 23, 24, 26, 30, 32–34, 148, 151, 154, 159

initiation, 60, 61, 63, 67, 149

interleaving, 122

Internet, 40, 124, 137, 147, 163, 167, 181, 182, 188, 190

interning, 160, 177

intoxicants, 142

investment, 20, 21, 23–25, 28–30, 40, 148, 152–154, 158, 164, 165, 173, 174, 176

GET MORE AT LLEWELLYN.COM

Visit us online to browse hundreds of our books and decks, plus sign up to receive our e-newsletters and exclusive online offers.

- **Free tarot readings** • **Spell-a-Day** • **Moon phases**
- **Recipes, spells, and tips** • **Blogs** • **Encyclopedia**
- **Author interviews, articles, and upcoming events**

GET SOCIAL WITH LLEWELLYN

Find us on     @LlewellynBooks
www.Facebook.com/LlewellynBooks

GET BOOKS AT LLEWELLYN

LLEWELLYN ORDERING INFORMATION

Order online: Visit our website at www.llewellyn.com to select your books and place an order on our secure server.

Order by phone:
- Call toll free within the US at 1-877-NEW-WRLD (1-877-639-9753)
- We accept VISA, MasterCard, American Express, and Discover.
- Canadian customers must use credit cards.

Order by mail:
Send the full price of your order (MN residents add 6.875% sales tax) in US funds plus postage and handling to: Llewellyn Worldwide, 2143 Wooddale Drive, Woodbury, MN 55125-2989

POSTAGE AND HANDLING

STANDARD (US):
(Please allow 12 business days)
$30.00 and under, add $6.00.
$30.01 and over, FREE SHIPPING.

INTERNATIONAL ORDERS,
INCLUDING CANADA:
$16.00 for one book, plus $3.00 for each additional book.

Visit us online for more shipping options. Prices subject to change.

FREE CATALOG!

To order, call
1-877-
NEW-WRLD
ext. 8236
or visit our
website

Brain Magick
Exercises in Meta-Magick and Invocation
PHILIP H. FARBER

Recent discoveries in neuroscience suggest that the magickal practices of evocation and invocation are related to natural brain functions—this book is the first to present a theory of magick based on the new research. The ultimate goal of invocation is to infuse your life with more excitement, meaning, and passion. *Brain Magick* is packed full of exercises that illustrate the principles of neuroscience and magick, and has everything you need to quickly develop skill in the art of invocation.

This easily practiced form of ritual technology is appropriate for beginners and advanced students alike. For those familiar with any kind of magick—Wiccan, Thelemic, Golden Dawn, Goetic, Chaos or Hermetic—this book will provide opportunities to consider their practice in a new light, and take their magical experiences to a new level. Even complete novices will be able to start immediately.

978-0-7387-2926-8, 264 pp., 5³⁄₁₆ x 8   **$15.95**

LON MILO DUQUETTE

LOW MAGICK

IT'S ALL IN YOUR HEAD . . .
YOU JUST HAVE NO IDEA
HOW BIG YOUR HEAD IS

Low Magick
It's All In Your Head... You Just Have No Idea How Big Your Head Is
LON MILO DUQUETTE

Take a fascinating journey into the life of one of the most respected, sought-after, and notorious magicians alive today: Lon Milo DuQuette. As entertaining as they are informative, the outrageous true stories in this one-of-a-kind memoir contain authentic magical theory and invaluable technical information.

DuQuette tells how a friend was cursed by a wellknown foreign filmmaker and how they removed that curse with a little help from Shakespeare. He explains how, as a six-year-old, he used the Law of Attraction to get a date with Linda Kaufman, the most beautiful girl in first grade. DuQuette also reveals the in and outs of working with demons and provides a compelling account of exorcising a demon from a private Catholic high school.

978-0-7387-1924-5, 216 pp., 6 x 9   **$17.99**

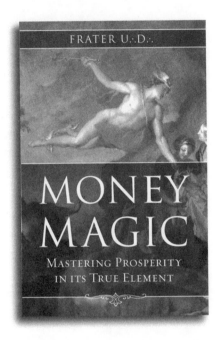

Money Magic
Mastering Prosperity in its True Element
FRATER U.:D.:

Europe's best-known ceremonial magician and contemporary occult author, Frater U:.D:., presents the definitive guide to money magic. Previously unavailable in English, this advanced guide will be welcomed by ceremonial magicians, mages, and hermetic practitioners.

Money Magic starts with the revolutionary premise that money is an elemental energy. By transforming the idea of money in your psyche, you invite wealth to flow more freely and easily into your life. This comprehensive course gives step-by-step instructions on how to master prosperity in its true element using new paradigms, magical invocations, rituals, sigils, and pathworkings.

978-0-7387-2127-9, 240 pp., 5³⁄₁₆ x 8   **$17.99**
